S0-CWY-613

The Beginner's Guide
to Small Business Computers

The Beginner's Guide to Small Business Computers

WALTER SALM

How to get your business-type personal computer with WordStar up and running in 10 minutes without an engineering degree or night-school classes in computers.

(Special note to nonreaders: you don't have to read this book; just buy it and turn to the Appendix for *the big secret* to 10-minute computer expertise.)

VNR VAN NOSTRAND REINHOLD COMPANY
New York

Copyright © 1985 by Van Nostrand Reinhold Company Inc.

Library of Congress Catalog Card Number: 84-15353
ISBN: 0-442-28032-7

All rights reserved. No part of this work covered by the copyright hereon may
be reproduced or used in any form or by any means—graphic, electronic, or
mechanical, including photocopying, recording, taping, or information storage
and retrieval systems—without permission of the publisher.

Manufactured in the United States of America

Published by Van Nostrand Reinhold Company Inc.
135 West 50th Street
New York, New York 10020

Van Nostrand Reinhold Company Limited
Molly Millars Lane
Wokingham, Berkshire RG11 2PY, England

Van Nostrand Reinhold
480 Latrobe Street
Melbourne, Victoria 3000, Australia

Macmillan of Canada
Division of Gage Publishing Limited
164 Commander Boulevard
Agincourt, Ontario M1S 3C7, Canada

15 14 13 12 11 10 9 8 7 6 5 4 3 2 1

Library of Congress Cataloging in Publication Data

Salm, Walter G.
   The beginner's guide to small business computers.

   Includes index.
   1. Business—Data processing. 2. Microcomputers—
Programming. I. Title.
HF5548.2.S185   1985   652'.5'0285425   84-15353
ISBN 0-442-28032-7

There is just one person who has made this book possible
—my very patient (and sometimes not-so-patient) wife,
B.J.—to whom I dedicate this book, with love.

Preface

You've just bought a CP/M business-type personal computer to help you do your word processing, mailing lists, forecasts, accounting, and bookkeeping. You've unwrapped the goodies and there it all sits on the desk staring at you. You stare back and wonder what to do first.

An old cliché says, "When all else fails, read the instructions." The person who first said that obviously had never had any experience with microcomputers.

The manuals and instructions that come with most computers today are an abomination. I'm convinced that they have been purposely written so that the only people who can really understand them are the ones who already know how all this stuff works in the first place.

The same is true of the manuals for most software (the programs that run on the computer) that you buy. In fact, the better and more popular the software, the more confusing the instruction manual is likely to be. Very few of them are self-teaching manuals with easy-to-follow tutorials.

True, there are some excellent self-teaching books available (*not* from the software companies) but none of them really say very much about what you really want to know right now.

All you want to do this minute is to plug in that new computer and start to use it right away. You don't want to spend the rest of your life studying manuals that are written in Anglicized Chinese, or spend your evenings in night school just so you can use your new computer.

This book won't make you an expert. I have purposely not gone into great detail or depth because you want to get moving. What we will do is get your computer up and running immediately.

You will find here specific step-by-step instructions on how to use CP/M*—a very widely used microcomputer operating system—and

* CP/M is a registered trademark of Digital Research, Inc.

WordStar**—the biggest selling business-oriented word-processing system. If you're like many of the people who buy moderately priced business-type personal computers today, you will probably have both CP/M and WordStar.

For more in-depth studies of the hows, whys and wherefores, you'll have to look in other books. Here, we are short on theory and long on nuts and bolts of how to make it work for you immediately. If that's what you're looking for, start reading.

WALTER SALM
East Brunswick, NJ

** WordStar is a registered trademark of MicroPro International Corp.

Acknowledgments

There are always people besides the author who make it possible to write a book. My special thanks go to: Ivens Stanton, who coerced me into buying and setting up a computer for his public relations firm when I worked there—at which time I discovered I really loved to work with the electronic monsters!

Gratitude and thanks are due to Bill Lederer, with whom I had many phone consultations over his own computer problems and questions. When my wife, daughter and I visited his wonderful writer's retreat of a home in Northeastern Vermont, he successfully twisted my arm and insisted that I write this book to make the world safe for business-type personal computers.

Special thanks, admiration, gratitude and lots of love to my wife, B.J., who as a trained programmer has been an invaluable aid to me on many fronts—including doing preliminary software screening for me for magazine articles—giving me more "free" time to work on this book. B.J. has also put up with my impossible work schedules, my emotional outbursts when frustrated, has run emergency errands to buy more computer disks, printer ribbons and paper, and most valuable of all, has been my very critical and sensitive first reader.

My thanks also to Bill Beach, who dropped by to visit and pick my brains about what computer to buy, and let me twist his arm into becoming my second reader.

And there's Ben, my big black Labrador, who kept me company in my computer room, and periodically interrupted me to take him for walks—giving me a welcome respite from the green screen.

This book was written entirely on an Eagle II computer, using MicroPro's WordStar word processor. Drafts were printed on a Star Micronics Delta 10, and finished typescript printed on a Daisywriter 2000—operating with a Consolink MicroSpooler external buffer.

Contents

The Beginner's Guide
to Small Business Computers

1
Unpacking the Monster

No doubt you've heard of Murphy's Law.[1] Unpacking the new computer is the very first opportunity you'll have to see Murphy's Law in action. First, don't let anyone unpack it in the shipping or receiving department. Have them bring that huge padded box right into the office where the computer will be used.

There are several reasons for this. The most obvious one is that if someone unpacks and transports the unwrapped and unpadded computer to another part of the building, you can expect that it will be dropped or otherwise clobbered. Once that happens, you'll have a lot of trouble figuring out why the beast won't run when you plug it in. You're going to have enough "fun" getting the system on line without having some clown drop it before you even have a chance to turn it on.

If you feel that the person involved is ultrareliable and never, never, never drops anything, then obviously, you haven't heard of Murphy's Law. Where computers are concerned, Murphy's Law takes precedence over *everything else.*

CHECK THE PACKING

The second important reason for unpacking the machine in your office is a corollary to Murphy's Law which says, "An important operating manual or set of instructions will be discarded by the Receiving Department." We could easily add another corollary to

---

[1]Murphy's Law (true originator unknown) states, in simplest terms: "Whatever can possibly go wrong *will* go wrong." There are many corollaries (secondary derivations or spinoffs) of this law that are especially appropriate to using computers.

this: "A crucial connecting cable will also be discarded by the Receiving Department, and its loss won't be discovered until the trash has been compacted and carted to the town dump."

Don't laugh; it's true, and it happens all the time—especially where computers are concerned. When *you* have finished unpacking the beast, check over all the packing material very thoroughly, and then check it all over again.

WHERE TO INSTALL IT

Now that it's unpacked and probably sitting squarely in the middle of your desk, the next question is where to install it. Answer: install it where you plan to use it.

Now if that seems too simple, stop and consider all the folklore you've heard about special rooms and air conditioning and white smocks and all of the other witchcraft where computers are involved. Much of it may be needed for some of the ultralarge maxi-computers that take up several rooms of space, but even those monsters are becoming more tolerant and humane in what they require from their human masters.

Plan to set up and use your computer at your desk. If you're not going to be the only person to use it, then set it up where everyone can have easy access to it—such as a special corner or an area that has its own typing table or computer pedestal table.

SPECIAL CIRCUITS

A microcomputer doesn't draw an awful lot of electricity, but what it does need is a clean, steady, *reliable* electrical supply. It can't have this if typewriters, coffee pots, photocopy machines, and other office goodies are plugged into the same circuit.

Try it, and you'll cry in anguish the first time someone runs the copying machine. Why anguish? Because the computer's ultrasensitive memory will be wiped clean of all those hours of work the first time there's the slightest glitch on the power line. This is called a "crash" and the idea is to avoid computer crashes whenever possible.

The first rule of thumb is to give the computer its very own electrical circuit—the same way you would with a room air conditioner. Yes, you'll have to call in an electrician and spend a couple of hundred dollars, but this small investment will pay for itself the very first week of operation.

The second thing you may have to do is to invest about $80 in a power line surge suppressor. This is a little metal box that plugs into the wall—and the computer plugs into the little box (see Fig. 1-1). It filters out "spikes" and other surges that can and often do happen. These spikes are called "power line noise" and they bedevil all sorts of intricate precision equipment. Again, it's a small, but very worthwhile investment.

Some of the more expensive computers may have one of these filters built into the system's power supply. If this is the case with your shining new toy, then obviously, you won't have to buy the little glitch killer. Find out from your friendly computer salesman. He should know, or should be able to look it up for you.

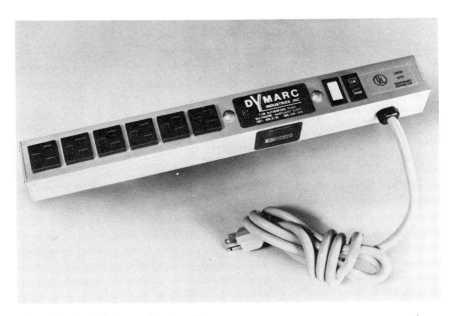

Fig. 1-1. (A) Stripline "Clipstrip II" power surge suppressor protects computers from power line spikes. (*Courtesy Dymarc Industries, Inc.*)

Fig. 1-1. (B) "Clip-Cube" power load regulator/conditioner provides transformer load regulation, line conditioning and isolation to protect computers from power line variations. (*Courtesy Dymarc Industries, Inc.*)

HOW TO KILL YOUR COMPUTER

There are several enemies to all computers and their storage disks. One very big no-no: beverages and liquids of any kind near your computer and/or its diskettes.

A liquid drip or a beverage spill can kill a computer and the stored data faster than you can blink. The repair bill can be staggering, and as for that lost data—well, that could just be priceless: Moral: keep those blankety-blank coffee cups and soft drinks well away from the business at hand. If you want a cup of coffee, don't keep the cup near the computer. Now that's fair warning.

Smoking around a computer may have little or no effect most of the time. But if some smoke particles get past the excellent built-in filters and into a hard (Winchester) disk system, you can kiss the disk and all of its files good-bye. Floppy disks are more forgiving of smoke and dust. Each floppy's inner jacket contains a soft "blotter" that is forever wiping the disk surface to remove particles as

Fig. 1-1. (C) Ambitious computer protection system provides uninterruptible power with sealed rechargeable battery system and will keep computer running for 20 minutes during power failures—long enough to save files and shut the system down. (*Courtesy Sola Electric, Unit of General Signal*)

soon as they land (see Fig. 1-2). But you have to wonder just how many dust and smoke particles this dry sponge can soak up. It does have its limits.

While floppy disks have some safeguards, there's an awful lot you can do to ruin them. For one thing, *always* handle the diskettes only by touching the outside (rigid) jacket. Never, never, never touch the diskette's recording surface which shows through an oblong slotlike hole on each side, and through a small round indexing hole (see Fig. 1-3). The same is true of the surface that peeks through the center spindle hole section. Don't touch!

Your fingers have a fine coating of oil on them—your skin's natural secretion and lubricant. Get even the tiniest amount of this on the diskette surface, and that disk is lost and gone forever—with all of its precious programs, files, and data bases.

Another enemy is magnetism. The disk stores information the same way a magnetic recording tape does—on a magnetically sensitive sur-

Fig. 1-2.   Inside each floppy disk shell is a protective "blotter" that absorbs dust and smoke particles from the air to keep them away from the ultra-sensitive disk surface.

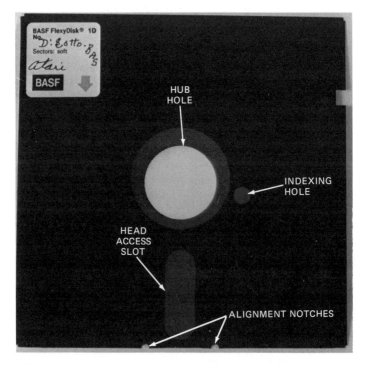

Fig. 1-3.   All floppy disks have slots and holes in the protective stiff cover. The oblong slot is where the computer disk drive "heads" read from and write to the disk. The tiny round hole is the indexing hole which admits a light beam that tells the disk drive where to find the beginning of the disk.

face. Magnets that are used to stick up bulletins on metal filing cabinets should be kept entirely out of the computer room or office.

Still another source of damaging magnetism is the telephone. Keep the disks well away from that bloomin' instrument. The same is true of dictating machines, loudspeakers, earphones, and microphones. They all contain magnets.

You have to label the diskettes, and there are special conditions here, too. Never, never, never write on a diskette's label with a ballpoint pen or a pencil. These will make indentations through the jacket and liner onto the diskette surface, and these minuscule indentations will ruin the diskette. To write on such a label, the *only* writing instrument you should ever use is a soft felt-tip marker, and don't bear down hard when you write (see Fig. 1-4).

More detailed labels can be prepared in advance in a typewriter or in the computer printer, and then stuck on the diskette jacket. Most blank diskettes come with a supply of these labels in the proper size and with the right kind of adhesive. If you use other labels, use *only* the peel-off self-stick kind, and never put them too close to any of the holes in the protective jacket—just in case you get a label that has adhesive "creep."

Fig. 1-4.   When you write on a diskette label, use only a soft, felt-tipped marker. Anything else will make a dent on the flexible disk inside and destroy data on it.

Avoid Heat

Heat can be another enemy. Never leave the diskettes where they will be in direct sunlight or near a radiator or other heat source. Some things get very warm—even the top of your computer, which is often a favorite place to stash those diskettes. Find some other place. Besides, you really shouldn't put *anything* on top of the computer except maybe a combination thermometer and humidity gauge.

We mentioned air conditioning before. The computer room should be comfortable, but you don't have to be paranoid about it. If it's comfortable for humans, it'll be comfortable for the computer. But in the wintertime, when the air gets very dry, you may have to add

Fig. 1-5.   Carpets are notorious for creating computer-crashing static. A semihard antistatic mat of this kind—laid on top of the carpet in the computer workstation area—will go a long way toward eliminating this static danger. (*Courtesy 3M Company*)

a humidifier of some kind, because dry air breeds static electricity, and this is another enemy of computers. This is one thing about which it pays to be paranoid.

Try to locate the computer in a room where there's no carpeting on the floor. If there's no way to avoid carpeting, you'll have to install an antistatic mat or carpet over it (see Fig. 1-5).

Keep a handy grounding point near the doorway. A bare metal lightswitch plate will do the job. People entering the room should touch this plate firmly to discharge any accumulated static electricity.

Also, silk and synthetic undergarments and outergarments are notorious for accumulating static charges. Try to wear cotton or cotton/polyester blends when you're around the computer.

If all else fails, keep a can of Static Cling spray handy. It's available in most grocery stores. Anyone who has a static problem should be sprayed top to bottom, front and back—*outside* the computer room before being allowed to go near the monster. The stuff smells awful, and after one or two treatments, people tend to start wearing cotton clothing to the office.

WHAT KIND OF DESK?

The desk or working surface for the computer should be made of wood or wood laminates. You probably can't avoid getting one with a steel frame, but all-metal desks and cabinets should be avoided at all costs. The metal cabinet acts like a big receiving antenna and storage capacitor for static electricity, and after the buildup reaches a certain level, it can zap the computer.

If possible, try to buy a desk that's made specifically for the computer (see Fig. 1-6). Get a *separate* stand or table for the printer. There are several reasons for this. First, the printer stand has special design features such as a paper feed slot for continuous forms, and feed and catch shelves or baskets for the paper.

Also, when a printer's running at top speed and you're at the computer trying to keystroke more data, you don't need the rattling, shaking, and vibration produced by most printers. You might even want to get a soundproof cover for the printer if the noise gets to be a problem.

Fig. 1-6. (A) Your computer corner can benefit from an ambitious assemblage like this: computer table with storage area pedestal, small removable hutch-top shelf for monitor, and a three-bin printer stand with slotted top—all connected by right-angle corner piece. (*Courtesy O'Sullivan Industries*)

Fig. 1-6. (B) If your needs are less ambitious, or space is at a premium, a compact, all-in-one workstation like this one may do the job for you. Note that it has room for the computer, monitor, two disk drives and printer. If you're using an upright, all-in-one computer, the hutch top can be removed to make more room. (*Courtesy Gusdorf Corporation*)

10

Fig. 1-6. (C)   This ergonomic workstation has electric-motor-driven height adjustments and an up/down tilt adjustment for the monitor surface. This type of workstation is more expensive than the wood furniture types in Fig. 1-6 (A) and (B), but may be necessary for some office situations. (*Courtesy Data-Mate/Maine Manufacturing Co.*)

If all this sounds like a bit much, you can ignore any or all of this advice completely. Your microcomputer will still perform—for a while. But things start to add up; the no-nos have a cumulative effect, and then one day, your computer will have a crash to end all crashes. Since Murphy's Law will still be very much in operation, this super-crash will happen just when you're in the middle of a top-priority project that has to be completed the day before yesterday. You don't need anyone to tell you that you can't afford to have this happen.

2
The Keyboard

Your first look at a computer—no matter what kind it is—can be a little unnerving. One of the first things you'll notice is that the keyboard looks different. Sure, there are a lot of similarities to the old familiar IBM Selectric key layout, and there's some comfort in this similarity. But when you look closer, you'll see there are some keys you've never heard of before (Fig. 2-1).

Fig. 2-1. (A) The keyboard of a standard IBM Selectric typewriter doesn't frighten most people—yet most computer keyboards are very similar.

Fig. 2-1. (B) Typical of computer keyboards is the Kaypro. Note the separate number keypad—a definite plus when entering a lot of numbers.

Fig. 2-1. (C) The IBM PC keyboard is getting to be among the better known layouts, but many programmers and veteran users don't like the close spacing on the right, the misleading "International" keycap labels and the "F" function keys on the left side. It's all a matter of personal taste.

Fig. 2-1. (D) Of all computer keyboards, the Apple IIe is probably the closest to the familiar typewriter layout and is only one of many reasons for this machine's popularity. (*Courtesy Apple Computer*)

THE CONTROL KEY

Two special keys may hit you right off the bat. They're called "Control" (or "Cntl." or "Ctl.") and "Escape" (or "Esc."). These particular two are found at the left side of every keyboard (Fig. 2–2). The biggie where they're concerned: the Control key, which you use an awful lot, isn't in the same location on all computer keyboards, and it may not be the same size or shape. In fact, you'll find that some computers have it in such an out-of-the-way location that it's almost impossible for a touch-typist to get used to it.

If you plan to buy more than one computer, it's a good idea to get systems with the same keyboard layout, so when people switch from one particular computer or terminal to another, they don't have to relearn the thing just for the afternoon or week or whatever, and

Fig. 2-2.   The Control and Escape keys are two new ones that don't appear on any office type-writer that you may have used. There's no magic about them; use Escape like any other key, and Control like the Shift key.

then go back to their own computer station with its different key layout. This can get confusing, and is certainly counterproductive. Keeping this in mind, it's doubly important that you buy the *right* kind of computer the first time around.

The Control key works very much like the Shift key; you hold it down while pressing some character key to get that key to do something different. When you hold the Shift key down, it types a capital (uppercase) letter, or the symbol at the top of a dual-character key. When you stroke a key while holding the Control key down, that key *performs some kind of special function.* This could be something like moving the cursor (that blinking square or line that tells you where you're working on the screen); it could erase a character or a word or an entire line; it could call up a special menu; it could turn the printer on or off, and so on. We'll get into that a little later.

Just to keep the record straight, whenever we tell you to type **[Ctl]** something, it means to hold the Control key down while stroking the key (or keys) that follow the **[Ctl]**. Some of the software that you'll be using will use the "^" symbol for Control. Thus, in WordStar, when you see an instruction to type ^QP, it means hold the Control key down while stroking the letters QP.

Some computers vary in the way they respond to multiple keystrokes when used with the Control key. For example, when using WordStar in certain installations, you may be able to type **[Ctl]** K1 (to insert the place marker ⟨1⟩ in the text—see Chapter 7)—holding the Control key down while you stroke *both* the "K" and the "1".

On other computers, to make it work, you have to type **[Ctl]** K, then *remove your finger from the Control key,* and *then* type the numeral "1". Yet on that same computer, holding the Control key down for both letters **[Ctl]** PS may work. You can find out only by experimenting.

THE ESCAPE KEY

The "Escape" key is in some ways misnamed. You'd think that simply pressing this key would get you out of trouble when you've given the computer some wrong or messy instructions. What actually happens when you press the Escape key depends on the program that you're running. Like all else with the computer, it comes down to what the software expects you to tell it in any given situation.

Typically, if you call for an operation that the software can't perform, it may flash an error message, telling you why it can't do that particular job, and will end with a statement like: "PRESS ESCAPE KEY TO RETURN TO NO-FILE MENU". This is often the case in WordStar, especially if you call for a program overlay that you haven't purchased—such as MailMerge or SpellStar, which are listed on the menu whether you have them or not.

What's a menu? It's a list of different types of operations that the program or system can perform—usually with a special prefix letter or number. By simply pressing the key that corresponds to a letter or number, you select that particular operation from the menu. The disk will click and groan while the computer loads that particular segment of the program into its user memory (RAM).

REPEAT KEYS

Getting used to the keyboard may take some doing. Computer keyboards generally tend to have a very light, sensitive touch, and you'll find that you like some keyboards better than others. Also, almost any computer is configured so that if you hold a key down too long, it will repeat, and you'll end up with double letters that you don't want, or even entire strings of repeated characters. But one of the beauties of the computer is that you can erase ("delete" is the word most computers use) these unwanted characters with just a couple of keystrokes. That's another one of the marvelous time-saving features of the computer.

You'll notice some special symbols on the keyboard, such as "∧", "⟩", "⟨", "\", and "|". These are used in writing computer programs and have no function in the kinds of computer operations we'll discuss in this book. Two special bracket symbols, "[" and "]", do have a place in some CP/M operations which we will see later on. Your keyboard may also have "{" and "}" brackets, although many of these special keys may print as some other characters if you're using a daisy-wheel word-processing printer. It all depends on what characters are actually on the print wheel in your printer (see Fig. 2-3).

One symbol you won't see on the keyboard is "¢". It's rarely used today, so no one thought it was important enough even to bother to include in the table of computer letters and symbols. The result: there's no ASCII code for the cent symbol. ASCII (American Standard for Coded Information Interchange) is a code combination of eight bits (one byte), and each time you stroke a key, the keyboard sends the ASCII byte code for that character to the computer.

In spite of the fact that there's no ¢ symbol on the keyboard, you can still get it with an overstrike combination in WordStar by first typing the letter c, followed by [Ctl] PH, followed by a slash (/). The [Ctl]) PH makes the carriage on the printer *overstrike* one character—typing two different characters in the same space. On the screen, the cent symbol will look like this: c∧H/. This feature of WordStar is also especially useful in foreign language fonts (typefaces) for placing accents over letters, if these accents are available on a daisy wheel for your printer.

Another way to get the ¢ symbol is simply to buy a print wheel

American English Print Samples

```
QUADRO 15/20          Model AE-03
ABCDEFGHIJKLMNOPQRSTUVWXYZabcdef
ghijklmnopqrstuvwxyz0123456789:;
<=>?@[±]²_°¼½¶§³!"#$%&'()*+,-./¢

QUADRO 10/12          Model AE-01
ABCDEFGHIJKLMNOPQRSTUVWXYZabcdef
ghijklmnopqrstuvwxyz0123456789:;
<=>?@[±]²_°¼½¶§³!"#$%&'()*+,-./¢

PRESTIGE 10/12        Model AE-02
ABCDEFGHIJKLMNOPQRSTUVWXYZabcdef
ghijklmnopqrstuvwxyz0123456789:;
<=>?@[±]²_°¼½¶§³!"#$%&'()*+,-./¢

PRESTIGE ITALIC 10/12   Model AE-05
ABCDEFGHIJKLMNOPQRSTUVWXYZabcdef
ghijklmnopqrstuvwxyz0123456789:;
<=>?@[±]²_°¼½¶§³!"#$%&'()*+,-./¢

SCRIPT 10/12          Model AE-04
ABCDEFGHIJKLMNOPQRSTUVWXYZabcdef
ghijklmnopqrstuvwxyz0123456789:;
<=>?@[±]²_°¼½¶§³!"#$%&'()*+,-./¢

ELITE 12              Model AE-08
ABCDEFGHIJKLMNOPQRSTUVWXYZabcdef
ghijklmnopqrstuvwxyz0123456789:;
<=>?@[±]²_°¼½¶§³!"#$%&'()*+,-./¢

BROUGHAM 12·          Model AE-12
ABCDEFGHIJKLMNOPQRSTUVWXYZabcdef
ghijklmnopqrstuvwxyz0123456789:;
<=>?@[±]²_°¼½¶§³!"#$%&'()*+,-./¢
```

```
BROUGHAM 10·          Model AE-11
ABCDEFGHIJKLMNOPQRSTUVWXYZabcdef
ghijklmnopqrstuvwxyz0123456789:;
<=>?@[±]²_°¼½¶§³!"#$%&'()*+,-./¢

GRANDE 10             Model AE-07
ABCDEFGHIJKLMNOPQRSTUVWXYZabcdef
GHIJKLMNOPQRSTUVWXYZ0123456789:;
<=>?@[±]²_°¼½¶§³!"#$%&'()*+,-./¢

PICA 10               Model AE-06
ABCDEFGHIJKLMNOPQRSTUVWXYZabcdef
ghijklmnopqrstuvwxyz0123456789:;
<=>?@[±]²_°¼½¶§³!"#$%&'()*+,-./¢

SYMBOL 10             Model AE-10
∇∞Ψφ+<∧¶↑∏§Ω∂∿↓ℓΓΘΣ→Ξα∆≡Τ~αβΨφε>
λη↑πκωμνοργθστξ×δχυς 0123456789 (
₽⌡σˀ^†↑~-_ʲ{}≤≧◎® ±∫÷ʲ√|•⌐ = ⌐z

ASCII 10              Model AE-13
ABCDEFGHIJKLMNOPQRSTUVWXYZabcdef
ghijklmnopqrstuvwxyz0123456789:;
<=>?@[\]^_`{|}~!"#$%&'()*+,-./¢

WP 10                 Model AE-14
ABCDEFGHIJKLMNOPQSRTUVWXYZabcdef
ghijklmnopqrstuvwxyz0123456789:;
<=>?@[/["™_#°_'§+.!©,*"-$()%®†¶|&

OCR-B 10              Model AE-09
ABCDEFGHIJKLMNOPQRSTUVWXYZabcdef
ghijklmnopqrstuvwxyz0123456789:;
<=>?@[±]²_°¼½¶§³!"#$%&'()*+,-./¢
```

·Equivalent to IBM COURIER™
COURIER is a trademark of IBM

Fig. 2–3. Daisy wheel print faces are available in a wide variety of styles and in three sizes—very much like the choice of type balls for Selectric typewriters. (*Courtesy Daisywriter Div., Computers International*)

for your printer that contains one. There are a few such wheels for some letter-quality printers. Then, when you strike a particular key, such as the uppercase number 6, for example, instead of getting the "∧" that's on the keycap and appears on the screen, when the printer runs, it will print out the ¢ symbol, if that's where it's located on the print wheel (Fig. 2–4).

Remember, the ¢ symbol *will not appear on the screen*. Instead, a particular character, such as the ∧ may appear there instead—depending on which key you have to stroke to get that character from your print wheel.

```
! @ # $ % ^ & * ( ) _ + <  |
1 2 3 4 5 6 7 8 9 0 - = > \


Q W E R T Y U I O P

q w e r t y u i o p


A S D F G H J K L : "

a s d f g h j k l ; '


Z X C V B N M , . ?

z x c v b n m , . /


] } ((SPACE BAR))

[ { ((SPACE BAR))
```

Fig. 2-4.   Enter a Crib Sheet like this in your WordStar disk file to see just what is on the Daisy wheel that you're using in the printer. Different wheels have different character sets that can give you various symbols instead of the ones you expect or see on the computer screen. The physical arrangement of each line depends on where the special computer symbol keys are on your particular keyboard. (*Line copy of text illustration supplied by author*)

Sound complicated? It's not, really. It's the same sort of thing as getting a special character ball type element for your good old IBM Selectric typewriter. When you get some nonstandard type ball, they give you a crib card that shows you what letters to strike to get a particular Greek letter or mathematical symbol. By studying the sample typefaces available for your printer, you'll find type wheels that are suitable for your needs.

You may have to create such a crib card on your own. You can do this simply by typing each key on your keyboard *in the order that they appear* on the keyboard. Do the shift keystrokes (uppercase) for each key first. On the screen, it will look something like Fig. 2-4.

If you happen to be using a dot-matrix printer instead of the daisy wheel type, your printout will usually contain the same printed characters that actually appear on the screen—unless the printer has changeable character sets in its software. This is something we'll cover in the chapter on printers.

THE RETURN KEY

The Return Key is very special on computers. You almost never use it as a conventional carriage return. Instead, the key really should say "Enter" because that's what it's used for most of the time. When you type an instruction or command on the keyboard, the computer won't obey the command until you "enter" it by hitting the Return key. A few computer manufacturers have relabeled it so it actually does say "Enter," but even then, it can be confusing, since there are times when you will use it like a conventional carriage return key. The IBM Personal Computer and many of its clones mark this key with an arrow with a bent-up tail—just to make matters more confusing. Be careful; that key is potent, and if you hit it when you really don't want the computer to obey your command, you can open up a whole can of worms.

NUMBER KEYPADS

Many computers have a separate number keypad. This is a small auxiliary keyboard to the right of the regular keys, and it can be very useful. If you're entering a lot of numbers, using that calculator-layout keypad can save lots of time and mistakes for you. The numbers on it are the same as those along the top row of your keyboard. Those number keys are *duplicates* of the top-row number keys; they're not different (Fig. 2–5).

The same is true for special symbols that may be there, such as "." and "," plus some other commonly used keys: "+", "=", "*", "/", and "-". These keys are all frequently used in certain data entry operations, and very often in programming. That "*" key is used commonly in CP/M commands—and in programming languages, it's used as the multiplication sign. To programmers, the "/" (slash) is the division sign, and the hyphen ("-") becomes a minus sign.

On some computers, you may find certain frequently used symbol

Fig. 2-5. The number keypad is a real time-saver for numerical data entry, doing phone lists, and other keystroking that's heavily number-oriented. Some separate number keypads are more convenient to use than others. This one on the Kaypro computer, for example, also includes a period, comma, hyphen and an "Enter" key (equivalent to "Return"). Number keypad keys duplicate existing keyboard keys.

keys—especially the "*"—in strange places other than their usual keyboard locations. This is supposed to make your life easier, but if you've already spent half your working life as a touch typist, it can get a little confusing and annoying.

CURSOR KEYS

Some other special keys your computer may have are four keys with arrows on them. These are *cursor* control or cursor movement keys.

What's a cursor? The cursor is the little square or underscore that blinks at you from the computer's screen. It is at the *working* location—and anything you type will appear at the cursor position, pushing the cursor ahead of the letters and numbers on the screen. The cursor is where the *next* key you type will appear on the screen.

Sometimes you have to use the cursor control keys in conjunction with the Control key, and sometimes they might not work at all, or will do strange things. When these keys work the way they're supposed to, they simply move the cursor around the screen in the direction indicated by the arrow on the key. They don't always work this way simply because they are under *software control*. This means that the software or program you are running on the computer must have specific commands built in to make these cursor control keys work the way you want them to.

These keys can be a big help and time-saver (see Fig. 2–6). They may surround a fifth key that says "Home". This key moves the cursor to the top left of the screen, or "home"—instantly, from any location on the screen.

Cursor movement keys will work if the particular program you're

Fig. 2–6. Cursor movement arrow keys can take several forms, depending on the computer. They all take getting used to, so don't expect to become a speed cursor arrow user immediately. Photo shows cursor keys for Kaypro.

running in the computer contains the right command information. Some programs are written specifically for the computer you're using, or may contain special sections called "patches" which tell the computer what to do when these special keys are stroked.

Many computers also have special "function" keys that may be labeled "F1", "F2", etc. (Fig. 2-7). These keys generally can be programmed—again with special patches in the program—to perform certain tasks when they're stroked. The jobs these special keys can do may vary from one program to another, depending on what's been patched into the command structure. They can perform very complicated operations or relatively simple ones—again depending on the programs and patches inserted into the programs.

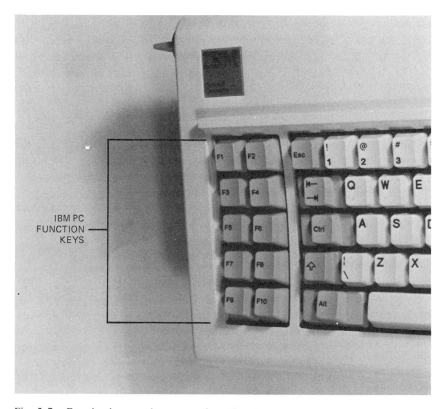

Fig. 2-7.   Function keys can be many or few. These keys are on the IBM-PC. Other, regular keys become "function" keys when used with the Control key for specific program commands.

BEING PRECISE

The computer is a dumb beast that happens to have a very high-speed electronic brain inside. The brain simply can't do its own thinking; you have to tell it what to do in precise detail. Thus, if you type the capital letter "O" when you really want a *zero,* the computer will think you want a capital letter "O". If you want a zero, you have to stroke the zero key—even though the capital "O" may look the same.

To avoid confusion, computer people write the numeral zero with a slash through it, so it looks like this: Ø. This is sometimes called a "Swedish zero" and the only reason this is done is so you can be sure it's a zero and not a letter of the alphabet. Some computer screens show the zero with a slash through it, while others may give it a special shape, such as a diamond—so you can tell it from a capital letter "O" when you see it on the tube.

By the same token, if you want the numeral 1, never, never, never stroke the letter "L." If you mean a numeral, then forget about what you learned in Touch Typing 101, but stroke the number key instead. That's what it's there for.

From time to time, you may give the computer instructions to do something destructive to a file or a disk. When this happens, many of the programs you're using will come back and ask if you *really* want to do that (Y/N). This gives you a chance to change your mind by forcing you to answer Y (Yes) or N (No) before the computer will go ahead and execute the command.

Thus, when you're running CP/M, and you say, "ERA *.*"—which means erase all files on the disk—the CP/M system will come back with the question, "ALL FILES? (Y/N)"—giving you a chance to change your mind.

Let's repeat that idea: THE COMPUTER IS DUMB. You must be very precise and correct in telling it what to do. You have to use commands that *it understands* and in a format that it will accept. The exact nature of these commands depends on the program you are running, since the computer can do absolutely nothing without that program.

This is not the time or place to go into a lot of details about programs (also known as software) and how they're written and used. Just keep in mind one thing: a program is a very special set of instructions that tells the computer how to do something when you give it specific instructions known as *data*.

A program is something like a professional chauffeur who knows how to drive his limousine, and knows the city's streets. You get in and tell him to take you to a particular address, and he immediately thinks of where that address is and the best and fastest way of getting there. He then drives you there. You, as the passenger, don't have to know a thing about the streets, how the automobile works, the traffic, construction delays, or speed limits. It's the chauffeur's job to know all this and to get you there. Essentially, that's what a program does for you.

By giving the address to the chauffeur, you have given him some *data* which he uses as his *input* for his program—which is his knowledge of the city streets, traffic laws, operation of the vehicle, etc.

The result of running that data through the program is the *output*—in this case, you arrive at your destination. If you give the chauffeur the wrong address, you get to the wrong place. If there's something wrong with the limousine and it breaks down, you get stuck somewhere between the data entry and the output. This can happen if a program doesn't work properly or the program diskette is damaged—but this shouldn't happen to you.

3
Don't Be Afraid Of Your Computer

The basic computer as it comes out of the box is a pretty dumb beast and needs some very special tender loving care and some oh-so-precise instructions if you want it to do things for you. For one thing, it's very intolerant of typographical errors, and if you make a typo when you keystroke a command, it will return that wrong command word with a question mark after it. For example, if you intend to use the command "TYPE" and type this instead:

A⟩TIPE **[Return]**

The computer will say:

TIPE?
A⟩

The same is true if you give it an instruction that's not in its vocabulary or in its transient program file.

Underlying this entire structure is a special kind of traffic policeman known as the *Operating System*—and in the case of your computer, the Operating System is called "CP/M"[1] which means "Control Program for Microcomputers."

Now before you go running for a cup of coffee or otherwise try to escape from this book, take note: CP/M is *your friend*. The Operating System will do lots of really terrific, time-saving and business-helping things for you with just a few taps of the keys.

---

[1]CP/M is a registered trademark of Digital Research, Inc.

Actually, CP/M is probably one of the most thoughtfully structured and thoroughgoing operating systems in existence for single-station 8-bit computers of the type you've just purchased. It's like a common language among members of its clan, and it's the nearest thing we have to a universally understood set of rules in the computer industry. You'll hear of other Operating Systems—such as MP/M (a multi-user version of CP/M), MS-DOS, OASIS, and UNIX—to name a few.

You'll also hear of CP/M-86—an advanced version of CP/M designed to run on 16-bit computers, and you'll hear arguments for and against CP/M wherever you go. But the fact remains it's used on more business-type personal computers today than any other Operating System. Because of this, there are thousands of CP/M programs available for you to use, and many of them are in the public domain, which means that you can buy them for practically nothing. CP/M is, however, now being eclipsed by PC-DOS and MS-DOS, the operating systems used on IBM and similar computers.

WHY CP/M?

The Operating System can also be something permanently embedded in the Read-Only-Memory (ROM) of the computer, but most business computer manufacturers let you have the option of selecting something other than CP/M if you want to. CP/M works with any computer that has a Zilog Z80, or an Intel 8080 microprocessor or similar compatible circuit (that's the "chip" you may have heard about) for its main processor—also known as a CPU (Central Processing Unit). This covers about 95 percent of all 8-bit business-type personal computers being sold today. This chip is the heart of the computer, but it needs something to tell it what to do, and that's where the Operating System comes in.

The chip may have some special commands built in, such as a reminder that you have to insert the System Disk in Drive A (see Fig. 3–1).

BOOTING UP

When you put the System Disk in Drive A, the computer will read the outer tracks on the disk which are reserved for the Operating System, and the computer will *Cold Boot* or *Boot Up*. "Booting"

Fig. 3-1.   Example of built-in screen prompt commands from the Eagle II that tell you to put a system disk into the computer.

is computerese for "starting," so don't let this word confuse you. You'll soon find yourself talking about booting up along with the most dedicated computer users.

When the computer boots up, it places that Operating System and its built-in commands in a special part of the RAM (random access memory)—the built-in user memory that's a part of every computer.

If you're using a typical computer, the RAM is most likely about 64K. When the system boots up, it will identify on the screen the version of CP/M that you're using, and in some computers, the screen will tell you how much user memory you actually have left— usually somewhere between 59K and 61K. The "missing" 3 to 5K is being used by the CP/M Operating System.

Next, you'll see that nice little A prompt (A)) on the screen with the cursor right next to it, winking at you. This completes the "booting up" operation. CP/M is now ready and awaits your command.

BUILT-IN COMMANDS

Resident commands that are always built into CP/M are: DIR, TYPE, ERA, REN, and SAVE. Let's look at DIR for a minute. It simply means "Directory" and when you type DIR **[Return],** the computer will print on the screen all the file names that are on the disk (see Fig. 3-2). This is a big help in finding out what's on the disk and finding a file whose name you may have forgotten. Besides, since you're a mere human, you probably don't keep a written log of your new file names; chances are, you leave that for your secretary or memory, or just trust to good luck. We'll get into the rest of the built-in commands in just a little bit.

```
A: PIP      COM : STAT     COM : DDT      COM : SUBMIT   COM
A: XSUB     COM : SYSGEN   COM : ED       COM : LOAD     COM
A: ASM      COM : MOVCPM   COM : DUMP     COM : ASSIGN   COM
A: DISKUTIL COM : DDISKUTL COM : ICPM60   ASM : EBIOS    ASM
A:          PRN :          HEX :          COM : CRUN2    COM
A: CBAS2    COM : XREF     COM : WSU      COM : INSTALL  COM
A: EXAMPLE  TXT : WSMSGS   OVR : WSOVLY1  OVR : MPMPATCH COM
A: WS       COM : ENV
```

Fig. 3-2. When you call for a directory (DIR), you get a display like this—and you can print it out by turning on your printer. (*Line copy of text illustration supplied by author*)

FIRING UP THE COMPUTER

Now comes the moment of truth. The time has come to plug in your new computer and try it out. For the time being, don't try to connect the printer to it. That'll come later.

You have found a nice, convenient location—possibly on the typewriter return shelf of a combination secretarial desk. Set the computer up there and plug it into that new dedicated circuit the electrician just charged you $300 to install.

Turn it on. If you're not sure where the switch is, look in the beginning of your user's manual, or just look behind the computer. Most of these machines have a rocker switch in the back (of all places!) probably tucked out of the way there so it doesn't get turned off accidentally (see Fig. 3-3). Turning the computer off before you've saved your programs and files can lose a lot of valuable information and/or keystroking time, and it can also possibly damage the floppy disks.

Turn the computer on and it will spring to life. If it has a cooling

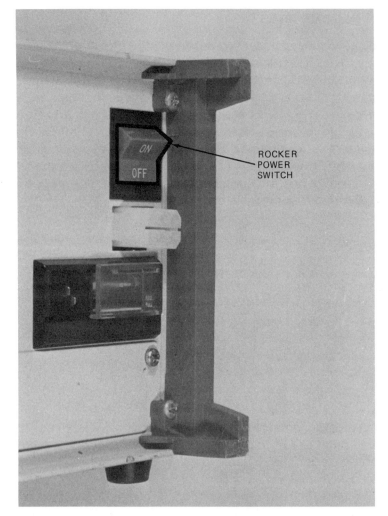

Fig. 3-3. The on/off switch is usually a "rocker" type, and is almost always "hidden" behind the computer—usually on the left side.

fan, it will start to hum quietly—almost apologetically. That's the *only* noise you'll hear. There will be no clicks or buzzes or musical beeps or gravel-voiced robots talking to you. A computer, if nothing else, is *quiet*.

A little green square or line (or white or amber depending on your screen color) will appear in the upper left corner of the screen and

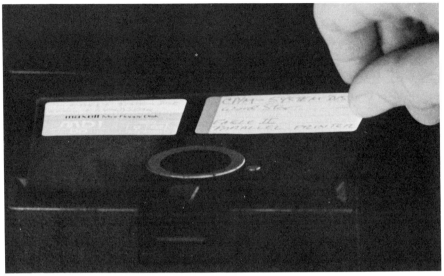

(A)

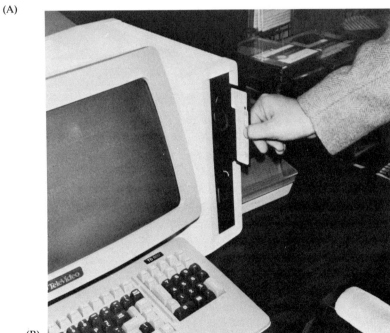

(B)

Fig. 3-4. Disk drives can be either horizontal (A) or vertical (B), but the horizontal arrangement is most common. In horizontal drives, the disk label must face *up;* in vertical drives, the disk label faces *left.*

start to blink at you. That's the *cursor,* and it's telling you that the computer wants some instructions.

Your computer needs its CP/M Operating System that's on the outer tracks of the CP/M disk that came with the computer. Slide this disk into Drive A (the upper drive slot if you have two horizontal drives; the left-hand drive if you have two vertical slots) with the label facing *up* on horizontal drives and facing *left* on vertical drives (see Fig. 3–4).

When handling the diskettes, touch *only* the heavy black cardboard outer jacket. Never, never, never touch the surface of the disk itself, which you can see mostly through the oblong slot (which is where the read/write heads make contact) and a little bit that peeks through the center hole. Slide the disk in carefully until you feel or hear a slight "click." That's far enough. Some computer disk drives may not give you this click. If that's the case, double-check with the instruction manual to make sure no click is mentioned.

Next, close the door. This can be a simple latch that folds down

Fig. 3–5.   These typical disk drives have two of the most common doors used—the flip-down type on the right, and the swing lever latch on the half-height drive at the left. (*Courtesy Shugart Associates*)

over the center of the slot, or it can be a drawerlike cover that slides down to cover the slot and clicks into place. It might be a lever at one side of the slot that you move through a 90-degree angle (see Fig. 3-5). In any event, the computer cannot read the disk or operate with it when the door's open.

BOOTING UP THE COMPUTER

Now you have to *boot up* the system. We talked about a *cold boot* a couple of pages back, so you know that this simply means loading the CP/M Operating System into the computer's memory.

The way you do this depends on the particular computer you're using. Some of them have a pushbutton that momentarily interrupts the circuit and is labeled "Reset." This button can be on the back or on the front of the computer. Many computers have no such button at all, but expect you to stroke a particular key combination to boot the computer. Again, it's back to the instruction manual, but now you know what "Boot Up" means, so you know what to look for in the instructions.

Or do you? This particular situation is also known as a "Cold Boot" or it may be called a "Cold Start." So you have two other names to look for. If you're using a Zenith or Heathkit computer, you hold down the Control key and type the letter "Z" (for Zenith). If you're using the tiny Otrona Attache, you hold down the *right* shift key while you stroke the "Reset" key on the left side of the keyboard. If you're using a Kaypro or an Eagle II, you press the Reset button in the back on the right side. The Osborne has a reset button right up front.

On the Dynabyte, there's a big red spring-return rocker switch reset button on the front in plain sight. If you're using an Apple IIe with a CP/M board, you can turn it off and then on with the rear-panel rocker switch, or you can hold down the Control key, the open Apple symbol key and hit the Reset key. Or you can type "PR#6" **[Return]** or whatever slot number the disc controller board is plugged into. You need a lot of fingers to do the walking on that one!

Once you've hit on the right combination, there'll be a click and perhaps a groan or two as the computer reads the disk in Drive A. If you have successfully cold-booted the computer, you will see something like this on the top left of the screen:

Eagle CP/M version 2.2.C
A⟩

The cursor will be flashing just to the right of the A⟩. The "⟩" symbol is called a "prompt" and it means the Operating System is in place and the computer is ready for more instructions.

Now let's make sure you've got all the stuff you need on that disk. Next to that A⟩, type DIR and hit the Return.

A⟩DIR **[Return]**

The screen will scroll upward as it prints several columns that look like Fig. 3–2.

These are the *files* that are on the disk you've put in Drive A, and most of them are special CP/M programs called *utilities* that will help you to use your computer. The wide space between the two parts of each filename represents unused available characters. A filename can be up to eight characters long, followed by a period, followed by a three-character "extension." When you type it, it looks like this:

FILENAME.EXT

In the case of the files in your directory, a short filename such as PIP would normally be written as:

PIP.COM

The COM in the extension means that this is a "command" file, and to use it, just type the first part—the section to the left of the period—and hit **[Return]** to load this program into your computer's memory and start it running. But the DIRectory does not show the periods in its display.

For example, if you wanted to run PIP (it means "Peripheral Interchange Program"), next to the prompt, you would type:

A⟩PIP **[Return]**

The file would then load into the computer's memory and in a few seconds, you would get a program prompt—in this case, an asterisk (*). The screen would look like this:

A⟩PIP
*

That asterisk or program prompt is asking you for instructions. We'll look at PIP and how to use it a little later on.

USING THE "TYPE" COMMAND

The next command is "TYPE" and this is CP/M's special built-in command for printing on the screen. If you want to read something that's in a file without actually opening that file, "TYPE" offers a quick and easy way to review this material. Keystroke "TYPE" followed by a space and then the *complete* filename. If you want to review the contents of a file called "XYZCOR22.713", all you have to keystroke following the A⟩ is:

A⟩TYPE XYZCOR22.713 **[Return]**

The computer will then read the disk, locate the file called XYZCOR22.713, and will display it on the screen. If the file is more than 24 lines long (the usual display height of most computer screens), it will *scroll* past the screen like a long, continuous sheet of paper (see Fig. 3-6).

This may all happen too fast for you to read the file and decide if this is the one you really want. You can stop the scrolling action at any instant by hitting **[Ctl]** S. This will freeze the screen. To resume the scrolling, stroke **[Ctl]** S once again and you're on your way.

If you want to abort the scrolling action and get back to good old A⟩, type **[Ctl]** C, and this will stop the program that's running and will give you a *warm boot*. The file will be interrupted, and the A⟩ and cursor will appear *under* the last line that was printed on the screen. It'll be near the bottom of the screen instead of the top, but it means the same thing: the computer is saying, "I'm ready, Boss; give me something to do."

A *cold boot* happens when the computer reads the CP/M Operating System on the disk and puts it into memory. A *warm boot*

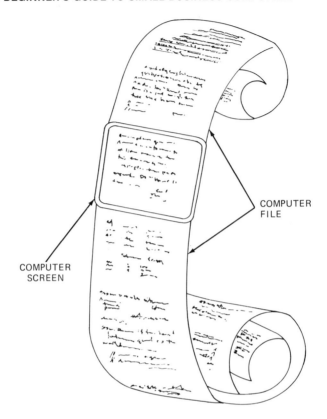

Fig. 3-6. The computer screen acts like a "window" that lets you view only a portion of a long scroll of paper (the computer file) at a time. You may "scroll" the window up and down and horizontally to view everything on that long paper roll.

happens when CP/M is already in memory; you're just returning there from some interrupted or finished program or routine.

TURNING ON THE PRINTER

By the way, if your printer is hooked up and turned on—which we'll cover in a later chapter—you can get it to type (print out) *everything* that you do on the computer when you're in the Operating System with one simple command: **[Ctl]** P. When you stroke **[Ctl]** P, you turn on a function known as "echo print"—the printer echoes everything that appears on the screen. If you make a mistake and backspace, it will print out your mistake *backwards* as you backspace.

Thus, if you mean to keystroke the command "TYPE" and instead stroke "TIPE", the printer will nicely record "TIPE" on the paper. If you backspace three times to correct the error, the printer will type each keystroke that is being erased in reverse order: EPI. The result will look like this: TIPEEPI. Then after backspacing to the T, you keystroke the characters "YPE", the *printed* line will say: "A⟩TIPEEPIYPE". All this because you made one little mistake!

If that sounds confusing, just remember that the printer can't backspace and erase the way the computer screen can. It can only duplicate what you actually stroke on the keyboard. That's why an electronic screen is so much more convenient to use than the type of computer terminal that uses a printer instead of a screen. If you want to turn off the printer's echo printing operation, simply stroke **[Ctl]** P again.

Very often, when you're in the echo print mode, the print mode will shut off when you run a transient program, such as WordStar. This is because the transient program takes over the computer's operating functions, and contains its own print mode. We'll cover printers in more detail in chapter 6.

LOCKED COMMAND FILES

There may be times when you're tempted to use the "TYPE" command to try to see the contents of a utility or transient program file. Some of these files will print on the screen, but they'll likely be in Assembler (machine) language which may look like so much Greek to you. Other times, you'll simply get a copyright statement and nothing else. This means that the program file is "locked"; it's protected so you can't see what's in it and perhaps pirate some of the program for nefarious or illegal uses.

THE "ERA" COMMAND

The "ERA" command (ERAse) is potentially very dangerous. You can use it to erase a single file, a group of files, or an entire disk, so use it carefully. As with DIR and TYPE, if you're on Disk A and want to erase something on Disk B, you can do one of two things: type "B:" **[Return]** to log into Disk B, which will get you B-prompt (B⟩) on the screen; or you can type a statement like this:

A⟩ERA B:XYZCOR22.713 **[Return]**

Even though you're still logged onto Disk A, this statement will tell the computer to look on Disk B and erase the file named XYZCOR22.713. But suppose there is a backup file as well. You would thus have these two files on the disk:

XYZCOR22.713
XYZCOR22.BAK

If you want to erase the backup file at the same time, you can use an asterisk (*) for the extension. The * is a "wild card" and equals *any* extension of one, two, or three characters. This is sometimes called an "ambiguous" file type. Here's how you would type it:

A⟩ERA B:XYZCOR22.* **[Return]**

This will erase two files: XYZCOR22.713 as well as XYZCOR22.BAK. We'll take a closer look at ambiguous commands and backup files in the next chapter.

When you use the ERA command, CP/M will not give you any acknowledgement about files that it has erased. It will just go ahead and erase the files and then give you an A⟩ (or B⟩) again. To check on what was actually erased, use DIR to look at the directory again.

RENAMING FILES

Another built-in CP/M command is "REN", or REName. As you may have guessed, this is used to change the names of existing CP/M files. Like most of CP/M, it's really quite easy to use, once you get the syntax (command word order) right.

Suppose you have a file named "OLDFILE7.713" and you want to rename it, calling it: "NEWFILE1.722". Here's what you do:

A⟩REN NEWFILE1.722=OLDFILE7.713 **[Return]**

That's all there is to do. You have just renamed the file. Try it out on some of your files. It'll give you a sense of accomplishment. When you've finished, type the DIR command to see the new file names.

As with any command, if you want to operate on something that's on Disk B while you're running on Drive A, you can do one of two things:
If you're on Disk A and want to rename files that are on Disk B, type "B:" [Return] to log into Disk B, which will get you B-prompt (B⟩) on the screen; or you can type a statement like this:

A⟩REN B:NEWFILE1.722 = B:OLDFILE7.713 [Return]

This kind of statement uses the B: as part of the file name, although to the computer it simply means, look on Disk B for the file and rename it on that same disk. The Disk Drive letter followed by a colon will *always* work in CP/M, no matter what operation you're performing.

The fifth built-in command is "SAVE," but its use isn't really important to you at this point and involves using transient programs which we'll look at later. For now, concentrate on learning to use DIR, TYPE, ERA, and REN.

TRANSIENT COMMANDS

Before you go off and hide, that word "Transient" isn't really so bad. What it means is you're going to use a CP/M program that's just too big to cram into the small amount of storage space that's allotted to the Operating System. These commands are listed as program files with "COM" extensions in the directory. They include such commands as FORMAT, SYSGEN, PIP, and STAT. You've already seen some uses for these commands, so they shouldn't be too awfully hard to understand.

The FORMAT command is used when you prepare a new, virgin disk so your computer can use it. We'll look at this in the next chapter, when we learn how to prepare a new disk for the computer. But that command file *must* be on the System Disk that you're using to prepare other disks.

When you type FORMAT [Return], your computer *loads* the FORMAT program into the TPA (Transient Program Area) of the computer's memory, and then asks you questions about how it should proceed. When you're through formatting, you hit the Return again to warm boot the computer, and good old A⟩ appears on the screen once again. The same is true when you run the SYS-GEN.COM program.

Using PIP to Copy Files

Using PIP is just a little different. If you load this program by typing PIP **[Return]**, the program will load and will then give you a *program prompt,* which is an asterisk (*). When you see this asterisk, you have to give the computer some instruction, like copying a file named XYZCOR22.713 from Disk A onto Disk B. It will look like this:

A〉PIP **[Return]**
*

Then type:

*B: = A:XYZCOR22.713 **[Return]**
*

Be careful! Use no spaces! Be sure to use colons (:), *not* semicolons (;) after each Disk Drive letter designation. With PIP, you always put the destination disk first and the source disk second in the equation.

After you have copied the file successfully, the PIP program will give you another * prompt asking you for more instructions. You can then tell it to copy another file, and so on. When you're finished with making all your file copies and are faced with still another system prompt (*), simply stroke the Return key *without typing anything.* The PIP program will be erased from the computer memory, and you'll get good old A〉 on the screen once again.

Using "STAT"

The STAT (STATus) command is another transient program command that we use quite a bit. It's actually quite powerful and can do a number of things for us.

If you simply type STAT **[Return]**, the computer will examine the disk in the logged drive (assume it's Drive A) and will tell you how much space is left and available to use on Disk A.

A⟩STAT **[Return]**
Bytes Remaining On A: 116K

or something similar.
   If you type this:

A⟩STAT B: **[Return]**

the computer will answer in one of two ways:

Bytes Remaining On B: 284K

or it may say something like:

A:R/W SPACE: 116K
B:R/W SPACE: 284K

   Getting the computer to read both disks at the same time is generally difficult to do. It's almost as though the computer has a mind of its own where this operation is concerned. Sometimes it displays the status of both disks; sometimes it doesn't. It all depends on the mood your computer is in.
   You can also ask STAT to give you more specific information, such as a particular file size. To request this information about the file named PIP.COM, type this:

A⟩STAT PIP.COM **[Return]**

The computer will answer with this:

Recs   Bytes   Ext Acc
  58   8k   1 R/W A:PIP.COM

Translation: Recs is Records, and a Record is 128 bytes long—the length or space available on one track in one sector. If you multiply

58 by 128, you get 7424 (bytes), which in effect takes up 8K (8,000) bytes of space on the disk—the figure under the heading "Bytes."

The heading "Ext" is an abbreviation for "Extents." An Extent is a single chunk or block of storage on the diskette. Really long files take up more than one of these Extents (they hold up to 16K each). In the PIP.COM file, the entire file is in one Extent or block, so the computer doesn't have to go looking for the rest of it in another Extent. No matter. You have no control over how the computer stores these files, and it's very efficient at finding continuations when they exist.

The "Acc" abbreviation means "Access," and under it the computer will display either "R/W" (read/write) or "R/O" (read only). Read/write means that you can both read the file, and you can change it or erase it. Read/only means that the file is *write protected* so you can read it but can't change it in any way. You can use the STAT command to write-protect individual files if you want to. Here's how to write-protect the file named XYZCOR22.723:

A>STAT XYZCOR22.723 $R/O **[Return]**

The file will now be write-protected, and if you call it up with a STAT command:

A>STAT XYZCOR22.723 **[Return]**

it will display this:

Recs Bytes Ext Acc
27   4k   1 R/O A:XYZCOR22.723

You can change a file from R/O to R/W or vice versa at any time with the STAT command. It all depends on which one you type following that $ sign.

Suppose you want to see a detailed record of *all* files on a disk. You can type this:

A>STAT *.* **[Return]**

You'll then see a display that looks something like this:

Recs	Bytes	Ext Acc
45	6k	1 R/W A:XYZCOR23.723
42	6k	1 R/W A:XYZCOR23.BAK
67	10k	1 R/W A:BLUENUN2.625
67	10k	1 R/W A:BLUENUN2.BAK
58	8k	1 R/W A:PIP.COM
41	6k	1 R/W A:STAT.COM

Bytes Remaining On A: 338k

And, as with all commands from the Operating System, you can get a printed record of the whole thing by simply stroking [Ctl] P before you type in any commands.

STAT will also lock up with the first "Bytes Remaining" number that it finds on that disk and will give you this same number over and over—no matter how much space is really on the disk—even though it's for a different disk. For example, if you STAT B: and get:

Bytes Remaining on B: 178K

then change disks and do it with the new Disk B, the STAT program will get lazy and not actually read the disk. Instead, it will tell you that you have 178K on B—even though you may really have 300K or 50K on that disk. The only way to get a true reading and get out of a stuck STAT situation is to *Cold Boot* using the Reset or whatever you use to boot up your computer.

4
Getting the Computer On Line

Now that you know the goodies are all in place, the next step is to make two *backup* disks so you can store this nice, clean, serial-numbered original in a safe, cool place away from your computer location for safekeeping. The reason: disks wear in use, and it's easy for them to pick up some dust or a magnetic glitch or two over weeks of daily use. Also, you may be able to combine several program files onto one utility working disk that will save you from having to change diskettes constantly. So here goes.

BACKUP DISKS

There is some confusion about backup disks and copying programs from one disk to another. As long as you own the particular program disk and don't plan to give away or sell copies of it to your friends, relatives and business associates, you are free to make as many copies of it *for your own use* as you want to. The software supplier expects you to do this, and in fact encourages you to do it so you don't pester them every two minutes to send you a replacement program disk for the one you somehow screwed up.

Formatting

Select a good quality blank diskette and insert it in Drive B and close the door. That new diskette is totally useless the way it is. It first must be *Formatted* and then have the Operating System copied onto its outer tracks. Formatting consists of laying down a series of magnetic boundary markers for the *sectors* on the disk.

If you've ever watched a waitress cut a pie in a diner or restaurant, you may have noticed her using a pie-sized plastic cover with a bunch of slots in it. She would put a knife through each of those slots and *mark* the top of the pie so each slice could be cut evenly and equally. She was dividing the pie into equal servings or *sectors.*

Disk sectors, if you could see them, would look like those marked pie slices, with the formatted disk resembling that pie that has been evenly marked into an equal number of pieces—but is still sitting in the pie plate, ready to be cut up and served.

Hard and Soft Sectors.   Most computers use what are known as "Soft-Sectored" disks. The black outer jacket has a small indexing hole near the large hub hole (see Fig. 4-1). The flexible disk inside has a similar hole which, each time it passes the holes in the outer jacket, lets a beam of light pass through for an instant. This beam of light tells the computer's *disk controller* circuit when this happens.

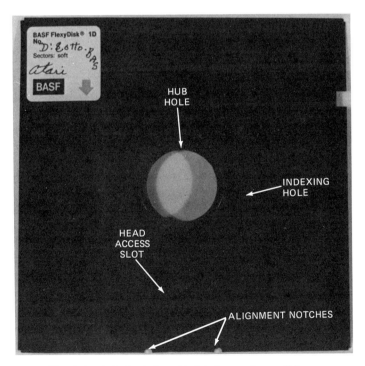

Fig. 4-1.   Indexing hole and hub hole on a floppy disk.

The controller then sets up the sector boundaries based on the location of this hole. This is what is called a "soft-sectored" disk.

Hard-sectored disks also have one hole in the jacket, but the flexible inner disk has 16 holes in it—each one defining a sector location. If a computer designer wants to put more sectors on the disk, he's out of luck. Very few computers use hard-sectored disks today, but you have to know the difference when you buy blank diskettes for your system.

Formatting the Diskette.   To start the Formatting operation, next to that A⟩, with many computer systems, you type the word FORMAT [*Return*]. This will load the FORMAT.COM utility program into the computer's built-in memory (also called RAM—for Random Access Memory). The computer will then start to ask for more information.

If the computer screen says: "FORMAT?", it means that your computer's manufacturer has given you a customized utility program with some other name. This utility can make your life a lot easier, but it's time once again to peek for a second into your user's manual (ugh!) under "Formatting."

The Kaypro and the Osborne, for example, have a utility named COPY.COM (see Fig. 4–2). To run this, enter the word "COPY" [*Return*] next to the A⟩ and then follow the computer's instructions. The Eagle II has a program called "DISKUTIL" which you type in next to the A⟩, and then make a choice from the menu that it displays.

Let's assume that your utility is a straight CP/M FORMAT.COM program. It'll say something like:

WHAT DRIVE DO YOU WANT TO USE (A OR B)?

Answer it with "B" [**Return**]. It will then say something like:

INSERT DISK IN DRIVE B AND HIT RETURN TO START

Do it. Then it may say something like:

FORMATTING IS NOW BEING DONE PLEASE WAIT

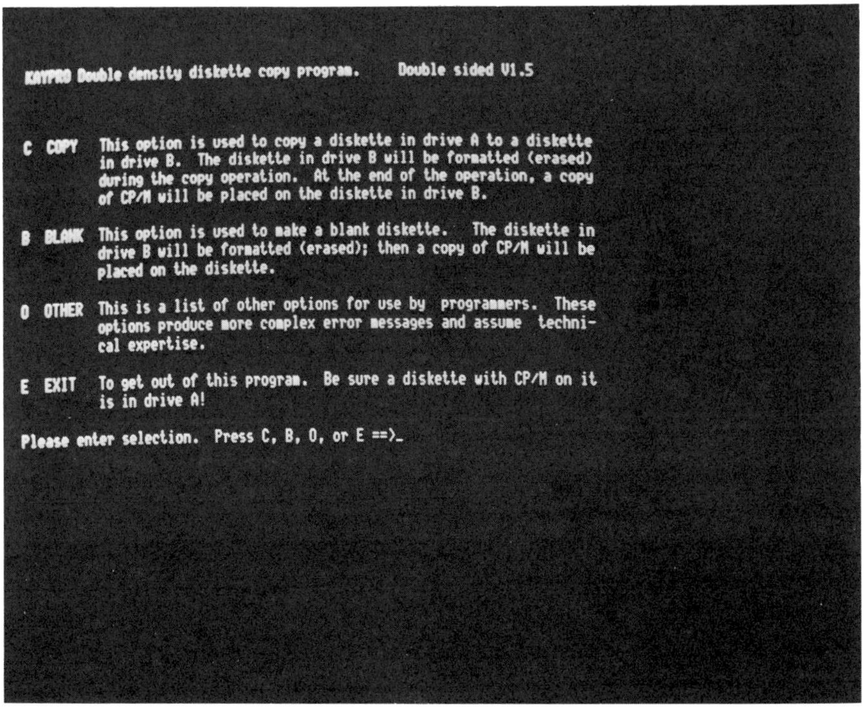

KAYPRO Double density diskette copy program.   Double sided V1.5

C COPY   This option is used to copy a diskette in drive A to a diskette
         in drive B. The diskette in drive B will be formatted (erased)
         during the copy operation. At the end of the operation, a copy
         of CP/M will be placed on the diskette in drive B.

B BLANK This option is used to make a blank diskette. The diskette in
         drive B will be formatted (erased); then a copy of CP/M will be
         placed on the diskette.

O OTHER This is a list of other options for use by programmers. These
         options produce more complex error messages and assume techni-
         cal expertise.

E EXIT   To get out of this program. Be sure a diskette with CP/M on it
         is in drive A!

Please enter selection. Press C, B, O, or E ==>_

Fig. 4-2. Typical copying utility program custom prepared by Kaypro, a computer manufacturer, to make your own work faster and easier.

Drive B will click in a rhythmic pattern as the computer lays down
the boundaries of the sectors on the disk. The screen may throw up
a series of numbers of letters—one for each sector completed. Other
systems just blink at you during the entire operation, and you can't
help wondering what the computer is doing and thinking about. It
all depends on how the utility program was prepared. When it's all
done, some sort of message will appear:

FORMAT COMPLETED O.K.
REPEAT SAME OPERATION ON A NEW DISK (Y OR N)

At this point, it's a good idea to answer "N" [Return]. You may
then get a message something like:

TO REBOOT, PUT SYSTEM DISK IN DRIVE A AND HIT RE-
TURN

Since the system disk is already in Drive A, simply hit [Return]. The
A⟩ will then appear on the screen.

Sysgen

Now that you have a formatted blank disk, it's time to add the Operating System. Next to the A⟩, type SYSGEN [Return].[1] The computer will then print a message something like this:

SYSGEN VERSION 2.2.B
SOURCE DRIVE NAME (OR RETURN TO SKIP)

Now type "A". With many computers, you will not have to hit the
"Return" key, but just typing "A" will start the operation. The
computer screen will then say:

SOURCE ON A, THEN TYPE RETURN

Hit the "Return" key. Now the screen will say:

FUNCTION COMPLETE
DESTINATION DRIVE NAME (OR RETURN TO REBOOT)

This means that the computer has loaded the Operating System from
the disk into the computer user memory, and it's ready for more
instructions. Type the letter "B". It will then say:

DESTINATION ON B, THEN TYPE RETURN

Hit the "Return" key again. Now it will say:

FUNCTION COMPLETE
DESTINATION DRIVE NAME (OR RETURN TO REBOOT)

---

[1]Some computers have COPY.COM programs that perform this operation automatically. It
may tell you, "Writing CP/M System to disk" when it actually does this.

GETTING THE COMPUTER ON LINE   49

Hit "Return". This will reboot the system, and the A⟩ will appear along with the flashing cursor. Disk B now has the Operating System on it.

Making Working Backup Disks

Now that you have a blank formatted disk with CP/M on it, it's time to start making those all-important backup or "working" disks.

Remember that we talked about "wild cards" (* and ?) in the last chapter? Here's where they really will come in handy. This is what the basic command line looks like:

A⟩PIP B: = A:*.*[V]

PIP is the copying utility, and it means "Peripheral Interchange Program." You then tell the computer that you want to PIP something *onto* Disk B (B:). That colon after the disk letter is *essential.* Now you are going to make it equal something else, so use the equal sign (=) and then the name of the source disk (A:). Again, the colon after the disk letter is a must. DO NOT USE ANY SPACES except after the "PIP".

Now you want to name the file(s) you want copied. Since you want to copy *all* the files, you use computerese shorthand. The asterisk (*) means all files, but the filename actually is in two pieces—eight characters (the filename), a period, and three characters (the filetype or extension). So you type *.* which means *all* files. If you wanted just the files that have the extension "COM" (the command programs), you would type: *.COM.

The [V] after the *.* is optional. This tells the computer to *verify* all the files that have been copied by checking them back against the originals to make sure they were copied properly. In a multiple-file sequence like this, the computer will list each filename while it's copying it. Naturally, longer files take longer to copy, and some are so long it will take the computer several passes from Disk A into the RAM (memory) and onto Disk B before the entire file is in place.

Here's what you do. To transfer *all* the files on Disk A to Disk B for a complete backup Disk, type:

A⟩PIP B: = A:*.*[V] **[RETURN]**

This simple command line will start a sequence that may take several minutes. The screen will flash something like this:

Copying-
PIP.COM
ED.COM
STAT.COM
etc.

The computer will click and groan as it first reads a file on Disk A into the memory, then reads that section of memory onto Disk B. Then it will go back and check to make sure it copied it correctly.

The PIP in that command line calls up a "transient" program stored as "PIP.COM" and loads this into a part of the memory called the "TPA" (Transient Program Area). You really don't have to know that, but you might run across this term in your later readings (see Fig. 4-3).

Go get a cup of coffee or go to the bathroom or something while the computer's doing this copying sequence. It'll take a few minutes. If you go for coffee, whatever you do, don't park the cup close to the computer when you come back. That's courting disaster (see chapter 1).

When it's all done, the A⟩ and the flashing cursor will appear under the list of files that have been copied. This means that the computer has completed the operation and is ready for more instructions.

Preparing General File Disks

Suppose you just want to prepare the disk for general file use, but don't need all those programs and utilities on it. You'll still really need two of the utility programs: STAT.COM and PIP.COM. So when the A⟩ appears on the screen after you've formatted the disk and put the Operating System on it (SYSGEN), type:

PIP [RETURN]

The computer will load the PIP program, and when it's ready, will give you a transient program prompt, which is an asterisk:

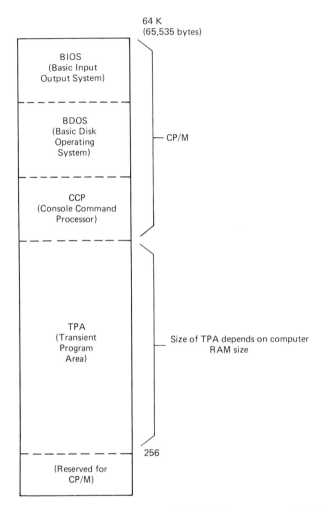

Fig. 4–3.   The user memory or RAM in a typical 64K business computer is divided into five areas. The tiny bottom CP/M area is reserved for the operating system's bootstrap section. The top three blocks are part of CP/M's "traffic director" section. The TPA is the part that you use. It holds your programs (such as WordStar) and the files that you create while using the word processor.

A⟩PIP
*

Doing it this way, you don't have to load PIP for each specific file, but instead can do it this way:

A⟩PIP
*B: = A:STAT.COM[V] [**RETURN**] (the [V] is optional.)

When the STAT.COM program file has been successfully trans-
ferred, the computer will give you another prompt:

*

Now type:

*B: = A:PIP.COM[V] [**RETURN**]

It will copy the PIP.COM program file. When it's done, once
again, it will give you a prompt, and at this point, the screen will
look like this:

A⟩PIP
*B: = A:STAT.COM[V]
*B: = A:PIP.COM[V]
*

Now simply hit the RETURN key; the PIP program will be erased
from the RAM, and you'll see good old A⟩ again.

This is a good time to make sure the two files copied correctly.
Type this:

A⟩DIR B: [**RETURN**]

You are commanding the computer to show you the directory for
Disk B (*always* follow the disk drive letter designation with a *colon*).
The computer screen will then do something like this:

B: STAT   COM : PIP   COM:

This looks very much like the directory we saw before for Disk
A, except that this one seems rather empty, since it contains just two
files at the moment. At this point, the disk in Drive B is ready to be
used for saving (storing) files of all kinds.

Labeling the Disk

Using a *felt-tipped marker only,* write some kind of designation on the label so you will know what the disk is for. Whatever you write, select an identification that you will be able to use consistently on *all* your diskettes so you know what it means three months from now. For example, you might want to print the letter "F" in the upper corner of the disk label to indicate to all and sundry that the disk has been formatted properly and has the Operating System and STAT and PIP files on it.

Then give it a number of some kind. If it's to be used for correspondence, try calling it something like "CS-1", and the next correspondence disk will be "CS-2", etc.

If different people will be keeping their own disks, their initials might become part of the diskette label—such as "WS-CS-2". This way, there can be no doubt at all as to whose computer or files the disk belongs.

Using the Labels.   Most packages of diskettes contain sets of peel-off labels that have space on them for writing additional information. If you need specific data on the diskette label, put one of these labels in a regular typewriter, type out the data you need (such as "CP/M Utilities and WordStar—Backup Disk No. 1") and possibly the date you made the diskette. Then paste this label next to the existing label on the top edge of the disk's protective cover (see Fig. 4-4). Whatever you do, don't let that sticky stuff touch any of the disk surface through any holes, and don't block any of the holes on the disk cover with the label.

This use of a working program disk in Drive A and a file disk in Drive B is the usual drill for most microcomputers. If, however, your diskettes have a very large capacity (500K or more), you might want to put the utilities and WordStar on *all* of your file disks. This can take up as much as 200K, but it can save you time and hair tearing later on. This will work *only* if you have lots of room on your diskettes, and there are very few computers that provide you with this much disk space.

If you have a more typical computer, you probably have 160 to 180K on a diskette (single-sided, double-density). With this kind of

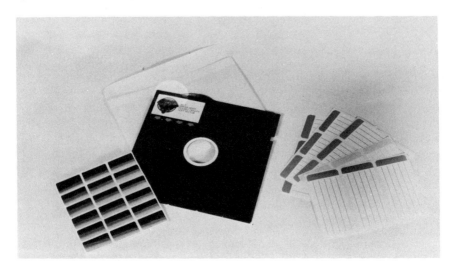

Fig. 4-4. When you put a label on the disk, use only the labels that come in the box of blank disks, and stick it on very carefully next to the manufacturer's brand-name label. These blank labels usually have enough room to write some key disk information such as disk identification numbers.

disk capacity, you *must* use Drive A for the utilities and transient programs (such as WordStar) and reserve Drive B for your files.

An extreme case is the unexpanded Osborne 1 computer, which uses single-sided single-density disks, which store just 90K each. With such limited space available, it's all you can do to get your basic CP/M, STAT, PIP, and WordStar on one disk, much less all the other CP/M utilities.

Extra Backup Disks

Now that you have your first backup disk ready and a file disk in place, make a second backup disk and keep it in your diskette file box. Your original program disks from the computer manufacturer and/or the software supplier should go into dead storage in a safe place other than at your computer location. Many people prefer to store these diskettes in a safety deposit box, because that way they're safe from fire or other damage. It's not that they're that valuable (except to you personally), but the idea is to keep them in a safe and temperature-controlled environment.

About those *two* backup disks: one will be your file master and the other will be your "working" diskette. If the working diskette ever develops a glitch or a program read error (and they *all* do eventually), do not use the master backup for anything except to make another working diskette. Do this immediately when trouble develops.

What About Guarantees?

You may have bought a batch of diskettes that carry a five-year or lifetime or some other ridiculous warranty. This is the manufacturer's way of telling you that if any of his disks have problem areas or develop errors, he will replace the defective diskettes with new ones.

Is this all a come-on? Hardly. But what good does it do you if the only way you can discover such errors is to lose some valuable files?

Keep this in mind and make duplicates of your file disks—each day or at the end of each business week—and put them into the bank vault, or another location away from your computer, along with those master program disks that are like gold. This provides you with the ultimate kind of protection in case of fire, flood, or any other catastrophe in your office. We'll go into the mechanics of this in chapter 14.

Write Protection

All blank diskettes are packed with spare labels, and some small black or silver-foil stick-ons (on peel-off backing). These little gizmos are for "write-protecting" diskettes. Every 5 ¼-inch diskette has a small notch cut out near one corner of the protective jacket (see Fig. 4–5). This is the "write-protect notch." In normal use, a beam of light passes through this notch. If you cover this notch by pasting a label over it, the beam of light is interrupted, and nothing can be written on the diskette. Also, nothing on it can be erased.

There's also a way of write-protecting individual files on a disk using the STAT command. This was covered in chapter 3.

For now, let's look at the first thing for which you'll use this command. STAT is short for "Status," and when the A⟩ appears on the screen, if you type STAT [**Return**], the computer will examine the

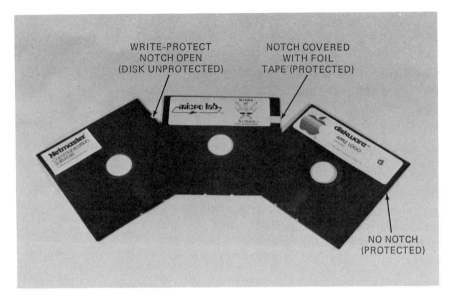

WRITE-PROTECT
NOTCH OPEN
(DISK UNPROTECTED)

NOTCH COVERED
WITH FOIL
TAPE (PROTECTED)

NO NOTCH
(PROTECTED)

Fig. 4–5. (A) The write-protect notch on 5¼-inch diskettes does nothing in its mint condition. When you cover it with the tiny square of black or foil tape that comes with the blank diskettes, the disk becomes write-protected and the computer will not be able to write (save) to this disk or erase anything from it.

disk in the A Drive, and will tell you how much unused space is still available on it. It may say:

Bytes Remaining on A: 160K

or it may say:

R/W Space: 160K

That "R/W" means "read/write" space: the amount of space you can still use for storing files. In computerese, "R/O" means "read only." This applies to files that have been individually write-protected.

Sometimes, the computer will throw up status for both drives:

Disk A: R/W Space: 160K
Disk B: R/W Space: 254K

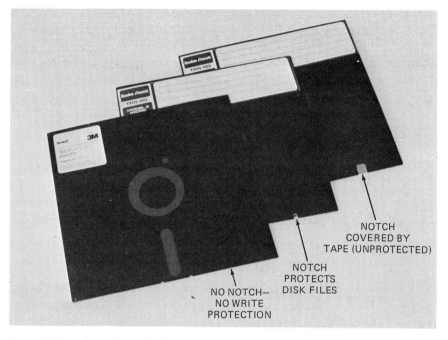

Fig. 4-5. (B) Eight-inch disks do not come with a write-protect notch and the notch works in reverse. To write-protect them, you must punch a notch in a precise location. Covering the notch with opaque tape enables writing and erasing again.

If you specifically want to find the status of Disk B and you have the A〉 on the screen, you can do this in one of two ways. You can type:

STAT B: [Return]

or, if you have the STAT.COM utility program on Disk B, you can *relog* to Disk B by typing:

B: [Return]

The screen will then change and say:

B〉

With B-prompt on the screen, any commands you enter will be acted on with regard to Disk B. But if you call for a program that's not there, the computer will simply question you about it. Suppose you call for the STAT utility and it's not on Disk B:

B>STAT **[Return]**

The computer will say:

STAT?

But it's not back to the drawing boards. In fact you can run Disk A's STAT command from the B-prompt this way:

B>A:STAT B: **[Return]**

You're telling the computer to look on Disk A for the STAT program, but to run it on Disk B. Or you can relog by typing:

B>A: **[Return]**

And the A-prompt will return to the screen:

A>

You can then type the STAT B: command and it will do the job. Either way will work. Just remember, the computer responds to commands only on the disk that is the *logged* disk—the disk for which the prompt appears. You can get it to read a command program into memory from a non-logged disk by telling it where to look for it—A:STAT B:. Also, remember, you *must* always follow the letter designation of a disk drive with a *colon*. Those are the rules with CP/M.

5
More System Commands and File Management

In the last chapter we mentioned some "wild card" commands that you can use with CP/M. Most system commands will work with these special wild cards—which are the asterisk (*) and the question mark (?). Let's look at the asterisk first.

This symbol can be substituted for *any* file name or file extension. If you want *all* files (each and every file on the diskette), you say: "*.*". That period in between the stars is the same period that appears in the filename: XYZCOR22.719.

You have to be very careful with something like "*.*". You can erase all of your files accidentally, and once you do, they're lost and gone forever. If you type the command:

A⟩ERA *.* **[Return]**

the operating system will ask you:

ALL FILES? (Y/N)

This gives you a chance to change your mind, because this is a very potent command.

Suppose instead you want to erase all the files with the BAK extension. You could type this:

A⟩ERA *.BAK

This will erase all the BAK files, and immediately will nearly double the available file space on your diskette. Just what are those BAK files, anyway? Let's have a closer look at them.

BACKUP FILES

One of the strange and wonderful things that CP/M does for you is to create automatically a backup or duplicate file every time you save a file (we'll get into SAVE commands later). This means that for every saved file, there is a duplicate file with the extension (or file type) labeled "BAK" (see Fig. 5-1). No matter what you may type in the extension of your file name, the extension will be replaced by the letters BAK in the backup file. For this reason, it's a good idea never to have two filenames with the same names and a different extension. Thus, instead of having two files named: XYZCOR22.713 and XYZCOR22.714, the second file should be named XYZCOR23.714. Two identical filenames will only confuse the CP/M backup system and you'll end up with a backup of the latest file you've saved, which will erase the previous backup file.

Every backup file gets the BAK extension, and you cannot read or print out from this file. If you want to use it, you must copy it in some way. Thus if you have a backup file named XYZCOR22.BAK and you've somehow damaged the original file, copy the backup with the PIP command, creating a *new* filename for it. Here's how:

A⟩PIP B: = A:FILENAME.BAK

Then rename the file on Disk B:

A⟩REN B:FILENAME.719 = B:FILENAME.BAK

This will give you a file on which you can read and write—which you cannot do with the backup file.

You can read or print out the backup file by changing its name—specifically the extension ("BAK") by using CP/M's REName command. To do this, type:

A⟩REN FILENAME.719 = FILENAME.BAK **[Return]**

B:	PIP	COM	:	STAT	COM	:	CHAP3V4	107	:	CHAP3V5	N07
B:	APPDX1		:	CHAP3V5	BAK	:	ILLOS8		:	ILLOS4	
B:	CHAP4V7	N11	:	HOUSE14	BAK	:	ILLOS3		:	BILL	
B:	CHAP4V7	BAK	:	TITLEPAG		:	CHAP3V7	BAK	:	CHAP7V2	BAK
B:	CHAP7V2	N12	:	CHAP3V7	N11	:	SHIFTKEY		:	CHAP8V3	BAK
B:	CHAP8V3	N13	:	DEDICAT		:	HOUSE14		:	SUPPLIES	

Fig. 5-1.   Filename extensions that say "BAK" are CP/M-generated backups and are duplicates of the original files. When you're finished with these files, you can do a little housekeeping
by erasing BAK files to make more room on the disk.

This operation replaces the lost or damaged main file, but in effect
removes your backup. If you want to create a copy from your backup
file, you can use the PIP command to work in the same disk. Here's
what you type:

A⟩PIP FILENAME.719 = FILENAME.BAK **[Return]**

This will erase the previous file called FILENAME.719 and copy
the BAK file in its place. If however, the reason for the lost file is
a disk error of some kind, *do not copy the BAK file with the same
filename as the old one.* It'll copy it in the same disk location as the
old one, and you can get the same disk error again. Instead, leave
the file with the error in place and create a new name or new extension such as FILENAME.721. This will leave you with two different
files called FILENAME—the one with the .719 extension that has
the disk error—and the new one with the .721 extension copied from
the BAK file.

If you're in WordStar, you can use WordStar commands to do
this, working right from the menu. If you have your system disk on
Drive A and your file disk logged at Drive B, do this:

From the menu, type the letter "O" (cOpy a file). WordStar will
ask you, "NAME OF FILE TO COPY FROM?"

Answer with: FILENAME.BAK **[Return]**

WordStar will then ask you, "NAME OF FILE TO COPY TO?"

Type in a new filename, such as FILENAME.719 **[Return],** and
WordStar will nicely copy the file for you into the new file slot. *Then*
you can read and write in the new file in the WordStar program. As
an alternate move, you can simply rename the BAK file using
WordStar's "E" command (rEname).

Using WordStar can be a lot simpler for some tasks, such as file copying, since it has a lot of prompts, and you don't have to re-member particular system commands or syntax. But we won't be getting into details of using WordStar for another couple of chapters.

Using the Question Mark

You probably never thought of the question mark (?) as a special computer symbol, but it can become a faithful servant to you when you use it as a wild card with CP/M commands. Suppose you have a dozen files that all start with XYZCOR plus a two-digit number plus various numerical and BAK extensions. Suppose you want to copy all of these files from Disk A onto Disk B. Here's what you type:

A〉PIP B: = A:XYZCOR??.*

CP/M will copy all those files and list them for you while it's copying them. This example uses two different wild card symbols—the as-terisk to match *all* extensions, and two question marks for the last two characters of the filename—*whatever they may be.* It will even work if there are blanks where those question marks and the asterisk occur.

These wild cards will work with such commands as: ERA, PIP, and STAT, and can be a big help in managing and reallocating your file space.

Setting Up File Names

There are no serious restrictions on what you call your files, as long as you observe the limits of eight characters and three characters for the filename and the extension. There are 12 characters that you can-not use as one of the characters in a filename, including a space. These are:

. , : ; = * ? 〉 〈 [ ] Space

Each one of these symbols has a special use or function, and you'd only confuse the computer if you tried to use them. Just remember—

they're illegal, but you still have 51 other characters that you *can* use—so don't feel that you're being cheated or shortchanged by the Operating System.

For example, you can't name a file XYZ*COR, but you can name it XYZ/COR if you like.

When naming a file, try to use something that indicates what the file really contains. That XYZCOR series can mean "XYZ CORrespondence." You still have two digits to use for numbering: XYZCOR01, XYZCOR02, XYZCOR33, XYZCOR57, etc. Then if you want to call up *all* your XYZ correspondence files, you can do it with one filename and wild card: XYZCOR??.

Dated Extensions

The extension is another matter. We have found it very useful to enter a date code there. Thus we could have all the XYZCOR57 for July 17 listed as: XYZCOR57.717.

If, the next day, you decide to make some changes in that particular file, you can copy it over and change the extension to 718. Thus *all the changes* will be in the file with the 718 extension, but you must also change XYZCOR57 to read XYZCOR58 in the new updated file—again to keep the CP/M Operating System from confusing the two files when it creates a backup file.

When you use a dated extension, you can make safety backup disks of all of that day's activities from Drive A to Drive B this way:

A⟩PIP B: = A:*.718 **[Return]**

This will copy all of the July 18 files onto your safety backup disk. This is a very useful time-saver, and if you start with this kind of file-naming system right off the bat, making daily safety backup disks will be a breeze.

Now suppose you want to transfer all the files dealing with the XYZ Company—correspondence, contracts, proposals, etc. onto a special disk. If you are copying going from Disk A onto Disk B, type the following:

A⟩PIP B: = A:XYZ?????.* **[Return]**

This will do the trick and you will now have a disk that contains only files for the XYZ Company—provided *all* the filenames start with "XYZ".

Suppose you want to see how much space is taken up by the XYZ Company files. Try this:

A>STAT XYZ?????.* [Return]

You'll see on the screen something like this:

Recs	Bytes	Ext	Acc	
45	6k	1	R/W	A:XYZCOR23.723
42	6k	1	R/W	A:XYZCOR23.BAK
67	10k	1	R/W	A:XYZCOR22.625
67	10k	1	R/W	A:XYZCOR22.BAK
58	8k	1	R/W	A:XYZCONT1.719
41	6k	1	R/W	A:XYZQUOT1.720
45	6k	1	R/W	A:XYZCOR35.723
42	6k	1	R/W	A:XYZCOR35.BAK
67	10k	1	R/W	A:XYZCOR25.625
67	10k	1	R/W	A:XYZCOR25.BAK
41	6k	1	R/W	A:XYZQUOT1.BAK

Bytes Remaining On A: 300k

Using Old Disks

There's no ready rule of thumb on just how long a disk can be used and reused. Generally, a good-quality floppy disk will provide a year or so of good service. Some companies are now guaranteeing their diskettes for as many as *five years.* Others are offering a seemingly incredible *lifetime* warranty. The trouble with that idea is that by the time you find out there's something wrong with a diskette, and you get a replacement for it, you've already started to lose some of your files.

If you have two or three diskettes that you use as your current working file disks, and back them up faithfully every day, or even once a week, you're pretty well protected. You'll start to get itchy about certain diskettes after you've been using them for a while, and when you get itchy, retire them and start to use some new ones. Disks are cheap—with 5 ¼-inch floppies typically costing $2.50 to $5.00 in quantity for decent quality and reliability. This is one place where it doesn't pay to cut corners on replacements.

When you're ready to retire a disk, it's time to decide which of its files you want to keep in your current files. Once you've made this decision, then PIP your copies and get that old disk put away for good.

At this point, you might also want to create a "Master Disk" of programs, utilities, and working files that you want copied onto all of your disks. If you have sufficient space on your diskettes, you might want to copy *all* of your software and special situation files onto each and every new diskette. This is especially true if, for example, you're using 8-inch disks (see Fig. 5–2) in a double-sided-

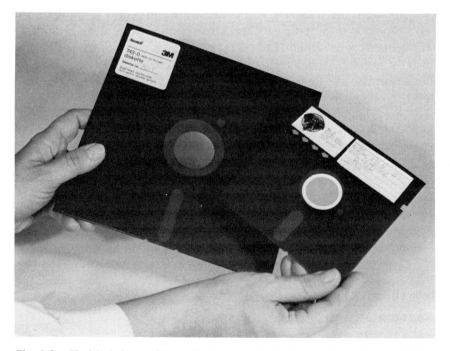

Fig. 5–2.   The 8-inch (larger of the two in photo) was the first floppy disk, and was an IBM development. The smaller, 5¼-inch "minifloppies" are much more convenient and easy to use and have become pretty much an industry standard today—even though they generally hold much less data than the larger disk.

double-density format. Such disks typically hold about one *Megabyte* (one million bytes) of data. So you can copy your CP/M utilities, WordStar, overlays and special files on each and every new disk.

Disk Capacity

The total capacity of a disk depends on the capabilities of the computer that you're using. You hear such things as "single-density," "double-density," "quad density," and "double-sided." Figure 5–3 shows the relative capacity of each of these disk formatting arrangements.

Older computer systems and some less business-oriented "home" computers use single-sided single-density disk formatting. The result is very limited disk storage capacity of about 80–90K. Computers like this are the Osborne 1 and most Atari and Apple computers.

Single-sided double-density track formatting is the most common arrangement in use today, but even 160–180K is very limited for many business applications. Ideally, an 8-inch disk with double-sided double density would be best, but 8-inch disks are rather unwieldy for desktop computers.

Using double-sided double-density formatting is gaining in popularity. However, there's one fly in the ointment; double-sided disks are awfully hard to get unless you order them in quantity (four or five boxes of 10 at a time) from a supply house. Chances are, you just can't go into a store and buy them off the shelf.

	TPI*	5 1/4 inch Single-Sided	Double-Sided	8-inch Single-Sided	Double-Sided
Single Density	20	80–90K	160–180K	250K	500K
Double Density	40–48	160–180K	320–360K	500K	1,000K
Quad Density	96	380K	760K		

*TPI = Tracks per inch

Fig. 5–3. Relative disk capacities vs. formatting arrangements. New technologies can cram as much as three megabytes onto a 5¼-inch floppy disk, but these aren't in general use yet.

Using Single-Sided Disks.   Many dealers and users feel strongly that a good quality single-sided disk can be used in double-sided machines with no problems. The reason: both sides of the disk have the magnetic coating. They're sold as single-sided because the disk manufacturer *certified* only the one side.

Certifying a disk or a computer data tape means that the disk or tape has been run through a special type of computer drive that writes a data bit on each and every available space in each track and sector, and then plays it back to see if it recorded properly with no errors. If an error shows up, the material goes into the reject heap.

Or does it? If both sides of a disk are checked on the certifying machine and one side fails, the other side is perfectly okay for single-sided labeling and sale. And this often happens. So if you try to use such a disk for double-sided computer disk drives, you're playing Russian roulette with your files and data.

The most difficult of all disks to buy are "quad" density—disks with 96 tracks per inch (TPI). This is very dense track packing, and not all disk manufacturers are willing to go to the extra lengths needed for tight quality control. Even when you buy disks certified and labeled for 96 TPI, chances are when you check them out on a 96 TPI computer disk drive, at least 20 percent of them will fail. This book was written on just such a machine, and because of the large disk capacity (380K per disk), the entire manuscript took up only three disks, with room to spare.

What's the answer? If disks like double-sided and quad density are so hard to get, does it pay to use such a machine? Yes and no. Because of the large disk capacity, you need only half as many diskettes and can manage your more extensive files very readily. Certainly if you're running programs that require a lot of disk space, it's a good idea to go this way. Just don't expect to be able to buy diskettes at the corner stationery or local computer store.

If your computer system is also going to be used for accounting/bookkeeping by other people, they'll need their own disks and systems, and such programs take up so much space that there's not going to be any room at all for your WordStar and such. These are cases where double-sided and/or quad density are really justified.

The idea is to keep all your eggs together in the same basket, no matter what the old cliché says. You're better off this way, since you won't have to go searching for your software when you need it for your own needs.

Preparing the Master

The Master diskette in such systems is used to prepare each new blank diskette. It should contain such CP/M utilities as PIP.COM, STAT.COM, SYSGEN.COM, FORMAT.COM, and all the WordStar programs: WS.COM, WSMSGS.OVR, WSU.COM, WSOLVLY1.OVR. If there are other special programs, such as the overlays for MailMerge and SpellStar, those can also be included.

Then, when your new, virgin disk is formatted and Sysgen completed, simply do the copy program:

A\>PIP B: = A:*.*[V]

and all those utilities and programs will be nicely copied onto your new disk.

Remember, this will only work if you have lots of space on the diskettes in your computer's system.

A few computers are set up so you can select the type of formatting arrangement—single- vs. double-sided, and singles- vs. double-density. Such computers, if they're set up for double-sided double-density disks, will also read any single-sided single-density disks you put into them.

Unfortunately, most computers aren't this versatile, although some of them—such as the Kaypro, Actrix, and Seequa, come with special programs that let you read disks from several other computer formats or will accept such special programs. The Kaypro, for example, comes with a program called "Uniform" which reads five other formats. An extra-cost option, Uniform 15, lets the Kaypro read 15 different disk formats.

Ideally, you should be able to do this with any number of computers, but most of them don't use a dense enough track spacing to make this feasible.

6
Hooking Up The Printer

The moment of truth comes when you finally decide to connect your printer and get it fired up. There are generally two classes of printers that you'd be interested in: *dot-matrix* and *letter-quality*. The dot-matrix type produces the typical "computer print" with which you're probably familiar (see Fig. 6-1). The print is made up of a lot of tiny dots which, strung together, form the letters and other characters.

The letter-quality type produces material that looks like it came from a typewriter. It uses "fully formed" characters that come from a daisy wheel or a type cylinder (see Fig. 6-2)—somewhat like the type ball in the well-known IBM Selectric typewriters and all of their friends and relatives.

In general, dot-matrix printers (see Fig. 6-3) are faster than letter-quality types, except for the very low-cost models. But for general-purpose office use—even including mailing lists—a good letter-quality (we'll call them all daisy wheel types, for convenience) printer can do double and triple duty. In fact, it can do just about anything you need, including those horrendous reports, tons of correspondence, personalized computer-generated letters, and even your accounting and bookkeeping ledgers!

But if high speed is your main need, then a dot-matrix printer can be your workhorse—at least for your mailing lists and bookkeeping and accounting. These printers can zip through a pile of computer files in no time at all, and make it all look incredibly easy.

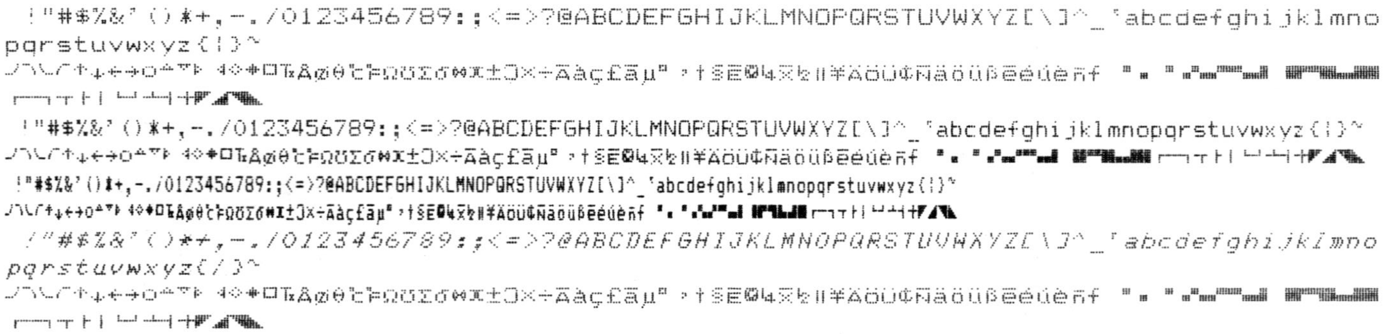

Fig. 6–1. Dot-matrix and Daisy wheel printers differ greatly in both the quality and the variety of their printouts. Here is a test turn of a Star Micronics Radix-10 dot matrix printer, and a Daisywriter wheel. Note the graphics characters created by the dot matrix machine. This type of printout is supplied by each printer's built-in self-test software.

```
!"#$%&'()*+,-./0123456789:;<=>?@ABCDEFGHIJKLMNOPQRSTUVWXYZ[±]²_°abcdefghijklmno
pqrstuvwxyz‡½¶§³!"#$%&'()*+,-./0123456789:;<=>?@ABCDEFGHIJKLMNOPQRSTUVWXYZ[±]²_°
abcdefghijklmnopqrstuvwxyz‡½¶§³!"#$%&'()*+,-./0123456789:;<=>?@ABCDEFGHIJKLMNOPQ
RSTUVWXYZ[±]²_°abcdefghijklmnopqrstuvwxyz‡½¶§³!"#$%&'()*+,-./0123456789:;<=>?@AB
CDEFGHIJKLMNOPQRSTUVWXYZ[±]²_°abcdefghijklmnopqrstuvwxyz‡½¶§³!"#$%&'()*+,-./0123
456789:;<=>?@ABCDEFGHIJKLMNOPQRSTUVWXYZ[±]²_°abcdefghijklmnopqrstuvwxyz‡½¶§³!"#$
%&'()*+,-./0123456789:;<=>?@ABCDEFGHIJKLMNOPQRSTUVWXYZ[±]²_°abcdefghijklmnopqrst
uvwxyz‡½¶§³!"#$%&'()*+,-./0123456789:;<=>?@ABCDEFGHIJKLMNOPQRSTUVWXYZ[±]²_°abcde
```

REV 1.08 VER 81
SOFTWARE PROTECTED BY COPYRIGHT
COPR. 1982
COMPUTERS INTL, INC.

DAISYWRITER Reg. U.S. Pat. Off.
        Marque Deposee, France
        Eingetragene Warenzeichen, Federal
                Republic of Germany

DAISYKEY (TM) is a trademark of Computers Intl, Inc. for a special protocol and,
DAISYPLOT (TM) is a trademark of Computers Intl, Inc. for special graphics.

SWITCH SETTINGS:
UUDDDDDD
UUUDDDDU
DUDDDDDU
L C 66

Fig. 6-1 (continued)

71

Fig. 6-2. Daisy wheels for different machines may or may not look the same. The Brother-type wheel (right), used in such printers as the Daisywriter, Brother, Comrex, and Dynax, is enclosed in a protective plastic shell, while a wheel for the Xerox-made Diablo printer (left) is totally open.

Fig. 6-3. The print head in this Star Micronics Delta-10 is typical of most dot-matrix heads; it doesn't look like much of anything and you wonder where the letters come from. Answer: a column of nine fine steel wires in the head which flies across the paper at breathtaking speed.

MAKING THE CONNECTION

Hooking up your computer to the printer is the first hurdle to overcome. If you bought your computer and printer at the same time from the same store, chances are the dealer will have supplied you with the right kind of connecting cable. But in case he didn't, or you elected to buy a printer later and separately, it's important for you to understand the differences between the connector types and what they're for.

By far the most common type of connector—also known as an "interface"—is the RS-232 or *serial* type (see Fig. 6-4). This is a

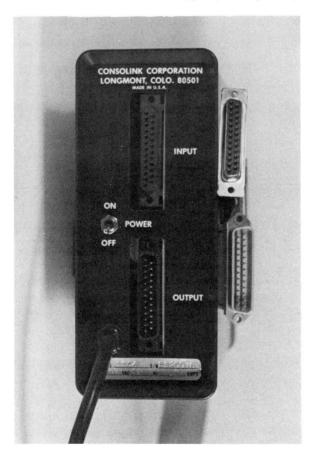

Fig. 6-4. Nemesis of all computer-users, the 25-pin RS-232 connector is used for making serial connections in most computers. The actual wiring for specific pin numbers may vary from one computer to another, so having a computer-specific cable made up by your dealer is a must.

"standard" type of connector that can contain as many as 25 pins. But only a few of these pins are usually actually connected in a printer hookup—generally no more than five of them. This is cost saving also, since you will need only a five-conductor connecting cable in such cases, and this is a lot cheaper than a cable with 25 wires in it.

The actual wiring of each connector in the cable can vary widely depending on the particular computer and printer you're using. For this reason, dealers will often have to make up these cables by hand for each customer, and such a cable easily can cost $50. Even if the dealer keeps these cable sets made up in advance and on hand, the price is about the same, because regardless of when his technicians do the work, it's one of those things that computers still haven't been able to automate.

The RS-232 is used for *serial* data streams. This means that each single bit—the smallest element of computer information—is sent one at a time through the cable on a single pair of wires. The rate or speed is called *Baud* and this means bits-per-second. We'll get into Baud rates and how to set them in a little more detail in Chapter 10.

Parallel Connectors

The Centronics-type *parallel* connector (see Fig. 6–5) is the other common type found on many computers and printers. This 36-pin connector is usually used "straight-through"—that is, pin 7 on the computer will go to pin 7 on the printer, no matter what—provided there are Centronics-type connectors at both ends.

Parallel in computerese means that data transmission is one *byte* at a time—or 8 bits. This requires more wires in the cable than serial transmission, since each of the 8 bits is sent at the same time, so each bit needs its own circuit. Generally, this type of transmission is faster and more economical than serial, but cannot be used with telephone hookups. Those *must* have serial for their operation, and are generally very slow—usually operating at 300 Baud or 1200 Baud.

While some printers may have both a standard serial and a parallel port, others may have neither one, but instead will use a special connector chosen by the printer manufacturer. Most typical is the edge-card type connector shown in Fig. 6–6. When you encounter this type of situation, all the rules about parallel pin numbers go out the window. Pin 7 on the computer could very well go to pin 11 on the printer, etc.

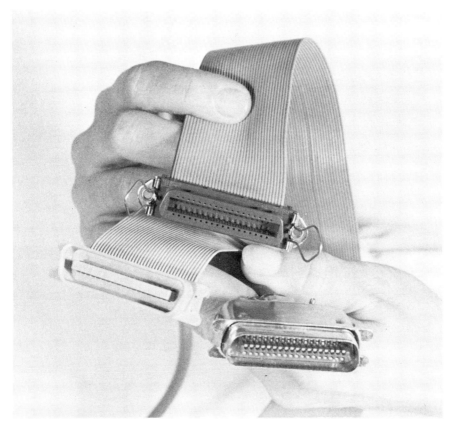

Fig. 6–5. The 36-pin Centronics-type parallel connector is much more standardized than the RS-232 serial type and is much easier for computer novices to use. Reason: parallel printer hook-ups generally work as they come right out of the shipping carton and cause fewer headaches.

The cables needed for such a hookup are very special, and may create a problem, unless you buy them from a dealer who sells *both* the computer and printer you own. There's no bargain involved here, either. It'll still cost you about $50.

Printing Garbage

When you first hook up your printer and try it out—possibly from the CP/M A⟩ symbol by stroking **[Ctl]** P, it may very well print out a bunch of garbage. This generally means that the CP/M printer "protocol" isn't right. Take a close look at the CP/M utility disk directory. Do this by typing: DIR **[Return]**.

Fig. 6-6. Edge-card connector on Computers International's Daisywriter printer takes special cable connector and has different pin-number connections than the RS-232 or parallel connectors. It's a dual-purpose connector, going to both serial and parallel computer ports. Selection between serial and parallel is made with DIP switch settings (see Fig. 6-7).

If there's a listing that says BAUD.COM, type BAUD [**Return**], and the Baud-rate program will load and come on screen. This is when you decide what rate of speed your printer will use to "talk" to your printer.

At this point, it's helpful to know what the printer's Baud rate is, if it's a serial printer. If the printer is parallel, then Baud rate is meaningless.

If you don't know your printer's Baud rate, then call the dealer you bought it from and ask. Or look in the (ugh!) manual and try to discover something if you can. Your printer may have one or more DIP switch banks (see Fig. 6-7) hidden somewhere behind a door or under a cover. These are special "protocol" switches, and they program your printer to accept certain kinds of data in a certain way.

Fig. 6-7.   DIP (Dual In-line Pin) switches line up behind front-panel door on Daisywriter printer. Settings of these switches is crucial, and once you get settings that work, keep a record of them. Many other printers make these switches virtually inaccessible, often forcing you to call in a service technician to set them.

You'll set these switches once and forget about them. In some printers, they're totally inaccessible without your doing some major disassembly work. This is because the manufacturer may feel that the switches shouldn't be fooled around with by the customer, but should be set by the dealer or a qualified technician, or at least someone who has read the operating manual.

If the dealer tells you to set these switches a certain way, do it. He may tell you that this will give you 9600 Baud, which is the most commonly used computer-to-printer transmission rate. If this is the case, then you have to call up one of your CP/M utility programs— either BAUD.COM or SETUP. COM or ASSIGN.COM—or whatever you have in your machine's utility package. Once you find the right place reset Baud rate, change it to 9600.

If you bought a "package" deal from a store, all of this should have been done for you before you plugged anything in. If it wasn't done for you, call the store and complain and insist that they send someone over to get your system on line. Even the Sears Roebuck computer stores will give you some help. If you bought the system at K-Mart or some other discount store, forget it. You're on your own.

THE FINAL SETUP

Somewhere in your CP/M utilities is a program for doing the printer setup that may be a special program created by the computer manufacturer. It can have some fancy or special name. Look once again at your computer CP/M utility disk directory (A〉DIR [Return]). Pick out the most likely sounding program files. The right one will have the ".COM" extension in the filename (see Fig. 6-8). If you're doubtful, just type the name of each file and see what it does. To do this, when the A〉 is on the screen, type the filename (omit the ".COM") and [Return].

If you get into a program that is obviously wrong, and you don't know how to get out of it, try a "warm boot" ([Ctl] C). If this doesn't reset your computer with A〉, you may have to hit the Reset button and get a "cold boot." In any event, you'll get rid of the program that you loaded, and you can try another one.

One of the perplexing aspects of doing this setup yourself is that the computer's CP/M utility for printer setup may expect you to select a type of printer from a list. If your luck holds true to form,

```
A〉DIR
A: PIP       COM : STAT     COM : DDT     COM : SUBMIT   COM
A: XSUB      COM : SYSGEN   COM : ED      COM : LOAD     COM
A: ASM       COM : MOVCPM   COM : DUMP    COM : ASSIGN   COM
A: DISKUTIL  COM : DDISKUTL COM : ICPM60  ASM : EBIOS    ASM
A:           PRN :          HEX :                COM : CRUN2    COM
A: CBAS2     COM : XREF     COM : WSU     COM : INSTALL  COM
A: EXAMPLE   TXT : WSMSGS   OVR : WSOVLY1 OVR : MPMPATCH COM
A: WS        COM : ENV
A〉
```

Fig. 6-8. Typing "DIR" may result in seeing a CP/M utility program directory printout that looks something like this. If you want it printed out, type "[Ctl] P" to turn on your printer before typing "DIR".

your printer won't be on the list, and there may not be anything that looks even vaguely similar.

Once again, it's back to the telephone and call the dealer, or better yet, call the computer manufacturer and talk to their customer service department. They'll tell you which one of the printers on the list is a "lookalike" for the printer you want to hook up.

No, this isn't cheating; it's just that there are so many different brands and models of printer out there, that there's absolutely no way the computer manufacturer can list them all. So you decide on one that "looks like" yours (to the computer) and will work the same way. Actually, this isn't so farfetched, since most computer printers fall into a half-dozen or so categories, and almost every printer in a category works the same as all of the others in that group. The units on the list just happen to be the most common printers that are in use.

Bells, Beeps and Buzzers

Every printer has some kind of "bell" built in. It's usually a circuit and an annunciator (loudspeaker) that makes an electronic beeping noise of some kind. The name "bell" is a holdover from the old-fashioned teletype machines that are still in widespread use. If a printer manual refers to a "bell," it's really talking about a beeper or buzzer, or whatever.

The bell signal is to let you know that something's wrong. It may just sound once with a single "beep," or it may be a continuous, unbroken wail, or it may cycle on and off: "beep, beep, beep," etc. It can mean several things, and some printers have signal lights that come on to tell you what's wrong.

The most common of these are: no paper, ribbon is out, cover is open (some of them have safety interlocks on them), or something special that is characteristic of that printer. The Daisywriter, for example, will beep and refuse to print if the paper lock is engaged (in the back position) when you're using a tractor feed.

Sometimes the bell means that the Baud rate is wrong and the unit won't print. Other times, when the Baud rate is wrong, the printer may work perfectly, or it may unexpectedly decide to print garbage. Printers often seem to have perverse minds of their own.

Tractor and Sheet Feeders

Probably the very first accessory item you'll want to buy for your printer is a tractor feed (see Fig. 6-9). This is an add-on device (in most cases) that is gear-driven by a gear attached to the platen. It usually fits over the platen assembly, and has two toothed wheels that fit exactly the holes in fanfold and continuous-form computer paper.

A tractor feed is very useful for printing out large files (like the manuscript of this book, for example) unattended. If you use a tractor feed and continuous-form paper, you can give the computer the print command and the system will do the rest; you don't have to stand there feeding individual sheets of paper into the printer, stopping to make sure each page is correctly aligned, and all the other good things you need to do with single sheets.

You needn't worry about the computer allowing enough space around the perforations for top and bottom page margins. Usually the software (WordStar in this case) will handle that nicely—sending signal codes to the printer telling it to "line feed" (move the paper up a certain number of lines) automatically. If your software doesn't do this, most printers have a "top-of-form" sensor which turns on and sets itself automatically when you turn the unit on (see Fig. 6-10).

Fig. 6-9.   Tractor or pin-feeds are usually accessory items that can be removed from or added to the printer. Tractor on top comes as standard equipment with Star Micronics Delta 10. Tractor on bottom is extra-cost option for Daisywriter.

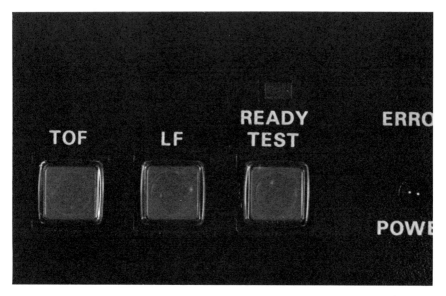

Fig. 6–10.   Most printers, such as the Daisywriter, have "TOF" (top of form) and "LF" (line feed) controls to advance the paper one full page length or one line at a time.

In either case, the printer is a pretty smart cookie and will do the job right for you if you give it half a chance. Sometimes, this may mean reading the instruction manual, even though it may be strictly against your religion. But then, computers really are dumb beasts, and we have to give them very precise instructions.

A sheet feeder (see Fig. 6–11) is often an expensive proposition, and before you buy one, be sure you have adequate economic justification for the purchase. The gadget fits on the top of the printer, and like the tractor feed, is driven by the gear wheel on the platen. It may also require a special electrical connection somewhere in the innards of the printer, and the installation, while simple, is best done by a qualified technician the first time.

You can remove the sheet feeder to make room for the tractor feed for those special times that a fanfold form is needed. But once you get a sheet feeder, you can do those hundreds of computer-generated form letters with ease and with very little supervision. All you need to do is keep the feed hopper full and remove handfuls of printed-out letters from the finished hopper.

Fig. 6-11. An add-on sheet feeder like this low-cost mechanical model on the Daisywriter printer, lets you use regular printed letterheads or plain blank paper without any need for bursting and peeling off sprocket holes. Finished typewritten pages come out the front and rest on the wire bin support.

Some sheet feeders have two feed paper bins for typing out two-page letters or documents. These will be neatly interleaved in the finished hopper. Other feeders are made for feeding envelopes, and some will do both paper sheets and envelopes.

A special control signal that will drive a sheet feeder has to be embedded in the WordStar file for some units. Again, it's back to the manual, or get the technician to show you what to do when he/she installs the feeder. It's really a simple procedure, once you know how.

Sheet feeders can pay for themselves in certain situations—especially those where you would otherwise buy specially printed fanfold forms with your business letterhead printed on the paper. This method is expensive, and requires someone to spend time "bursting" the fanfold after it's been printed. If this word is new to you, bursting means tearing apart each individual page on its perforations (see Fig. 6–12), and tearing off the pin-feed hole strips on their perforations.

Bottom Feed. Some printers allow you to feed the paper from the back around the platen (the conventional way) or alternatively through a slot in the bottom of the printer. This latter method is called "bottom feed," for obvious reasons, and is a lot easier to use if you're printing on fanfold paper.

Certain types of peel-off mailing labels *must* go through a bottom feed. The adhesive on these labels has such a low release point, that

Fig. 6–12. Using fanfold paper with a tractor feed means that at some point, some "lucky" person gets to burst and strip the paper into individual 8½ × 11-inch sheets. Here, the author's wife has been pressed into service.

if you try to feed them through the back of the printer, some of them will peel off inside the machine and generally gum up the platen and everything else. Unlike those in typewriters, the platen on some printer models can be devilishly difficult to remove for cleaning, so be careful.

If you don't have bottom feed, be sure to specify this to the dealer when you order your peel-off labels. The labels *must* be designed with a strong enough adhesive so they won't release from the backing during their pass through the printer. This is a bitter lesson to have to learn the hard way—especially right after you've purchased a box of 25,000 mailing labels.

Supplies

The last thing you worry about when you buy a printer are the supplies to keep it going, but they're important, and often expensive. These include replacement print wheels for daisy-wheel printers, replacement ribbons, and paper, which we've already talked about a little.

Some printers offer the option of using either a plastic or a metal print wheel. The metal is more expensive, but lasts much longer. Print wheels take such a beating that they do wear out after a relatively short time. A plastic wheel on a Diablo 630, for example, can require replacement as often as every two or three months in an office that places heavy demands on the printer. Keep a couple of replacements on hand *at all times*. The reason: just when you need a replacement wheel the most, the local computer store will be out of them and unable to get any for two months.

Also, keep a selection of different type sizes and faces on hand. You should have a least one daisy wheel in each of the three sizes— 10- 12- and 15-pitch. Keep extras of the one wheel that you use the most frequently.

Ribbons are another matter. You'll soon see what the use patterns are in your office. For starters, get a box of a half-dozen mylar (plastic) film ribbons. If your printer is the type that can take a reusable nylon (cloth) ribbon, get some of those too, and use them for draft copies. This will save you a bundle on those mylar throwaway ribbons that cost $7.50 each and don't last all that long.

Some printers present you with a very special gift: they don't re-

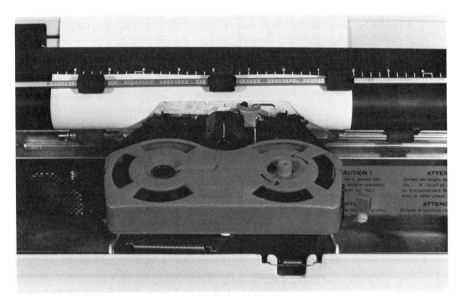

Fig. 6–13. Low-cost IBM Selectric typewriter ribbon is all that's needed for this Daisywriter printer—an important feature that can keep a lid on operating costs.

quire a computer-type ribbon cartridge. The Daisywriter, for example, uses a standard IBM Selectric II typewriter ribbon, which costs $3.50 (see Fig. 6–13). The Star Micronics Delta 10 is another machine that uses regular typewriter ribbons—in this case a standard nylon reusable type also available in stationery stores.

Ribbons like these represent a cost saving that should be considered when you buy your printer. If you've already bought your printer, this knowledge won't be of much help to you until next time.

No matter what the supplies cost, or how little you *think* you use your printer, always, always, always keep an adequate stock of spare printer supplies: ribbons, print wheels, paper, and labels on hand. You always run out of these things when the stores are closed or out of stock.

7

Making WordStar Your Servant

Getting WordStar into your computer is as easy as typing WS and hitting the Return key. That's all there is to loading this word processing program. But to do this, the WordStar must have been *installed* by your dealer. We're not going to go into the details of how to install WordStar here. It involves a special utility program on your master WordStar disk and means that the WordStar is set up to work with *your particular computer and printer*. It's best done by a computer technician, and if you're brand new to computers, *don't you dare* try to do it yourself.

When you load WordStar by typing WS **[Return]** next to the A⟩, the screen will go blank for a few seconds, then you'll see a display that looks like Fig. 7–1.

After a pause of a few seconds, the screen display will change, and will present the "No-File Menu" (Fig. 7–2). This is your starting point, and you can start any number of operations simply by typing the appropriate letter that's on the screen.

The very first thing you should do is *change the logged disk drive.* Do this by typing the letter "L." This is important because your disk in Drive A is the logged disk and you want to store your files on the disk in Drive B.

After you type L, the computer will say:

THE LOGGED DISK DRIVE IS NOW A:
NEW LOGGED DISK DRIVE (letter, colon and RETURN)?

So do it. Type:

B: **[Return]**

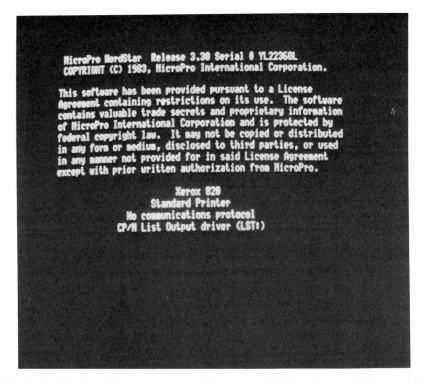

MicroPro WordStar Release 3.30 Serial # YL22366L
COPYRIGHT (C) 1983, MicroPro International Corporation.

This software has been provided pursuant to a License
Agreement containing restrictions on its use. The software
contains valuable trade secrets and proprietary information
of MicroPro International Corporation and is protected by
federal copyright law. It may not be copied or distributed
in any form or medium, disclosed to third parties, or used
in any manner not provided for in said License Agreement
except with prior written authorization from MicroPro.

Xerox 820
Standard Printer
No communications protocol
CP/M List Output driver (LST:)

Fig. 7-1.   The first display that comes up after you type "WS" and return, is this copyright
warning, and a listing of the hardware that you're using with the program.

Remember, that's a *colon*—not a semicolon. As with all symbols
(non-alphabetic characters), even if you have the Shift Lock or
"CAPS" key depressed, you *must* hold down the Shift key when
you type a colon. Otherwise you'll get a semicolon.

With some computers and some versions of WordStar, you can
get away with not typing the colon at all. Try it and see if it works
with your computer.

When the logged disk drive changes, the File Directory listing under the menu will also change. The new Directory will show the files
that you have on the disk in Drive B. Now you're all set to do some
word processing.

The first thing you do is to open a file. The menu command letter
"D" opens or creates a *Document File* which is the kind of file you
want to use about 95 percent of the time. "N" opens a *Non-*

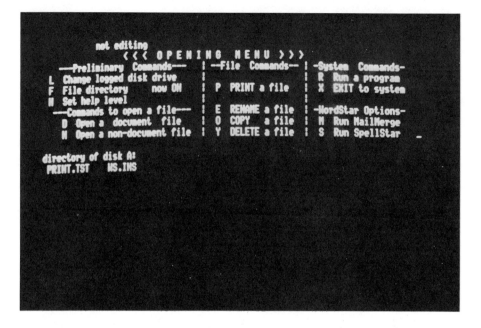

Fig. 7–2. WordStar's no-file menu is your starting point to the wonderful world of heavy-duty word processing. Keying any letter on this menu gets you on your way, but try "D" first. That's the easiest, since that will open a new or old "document file".

Document File, which may consist of raw data, name and address listings, and so on—things you would want to use along with a "Sorting Program" (covered in chapter 13) or with "MailMerge," which we'll be getting into in chapter 12.

You should use the Document File command D any time you want to open up an existing word processing (non-data) file or start a new one. When you type the letter D, the computer will ask you the name of the file. You then type the file name (up to eight characters, period and optional three-character extension), and then **[Return]**.

WordStar will shift gears, some new material will be loaded into memory from the program disk in Drive A, and one of two things will happen: the beginning of the file you named will appear on the screen, or the screen will flash the message NEW FILE.

Very often, even experienced WordStar operators will get the NEW FILE message when they really want to open an old file. It simply means that you didn't type in the name of the file you want *exactly the way it appears in the directory.*

If this happens, and what you really wanted to do was to open an existing file, WordStar has a quick shortcut to get out of there: **[Ctl]** KQ. You'll get the message immediately that the computer is abandoning unedited file FILENAME.XYZ. It will then return you to the No-File Menu and you can start all over again.

Remember, the computer is very exacting; if you type something, it assumes that what you typed is what you want. It would be nice if computers came with a "DWIM" (Do What I Mean) key. Since they don't, you have to be very exact in what you type. Computers only know how to do *what you tell them to do.*

WHY IS IT SO HARD?

WordStar at first may look very hard to learn. It's not. The trouble is that it's a program that is just loaded with special features and operations—many of which you may never need to use. We're going to look at some shortcuts here to get you up and running with WordStar fast.

When you open or start a new file, you'll see the *Status Line* at the top of the page. It's actually two lines: the status line and the top ruler line. In some versions of WordStar, it may look like Fig. 7-3.

But most of the time, when your file first comes up, it will probably look like Fig. 7-4.

The first entry shown in Fig. 7-4, B:PRACTICE.XYZ, tells you that you're looking at a file on Disk B named PRACTICE.XYZ. The second entry gives the page number. The third and fourth entries pinpoint the location of the *cursor*—that blinking square or little blinking line that is the place where you are currently working.

The line number is the line on the *printed portion* of the page, and the column number changes constantly as you type across the page to the maximum width. "Column" in computer terminology means "letter" or "character" number. Thus, if you've already typed 15

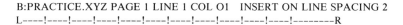

B:PRACTICE.XYZ PAGE 1 LINE 1 COL O1   INSERT ON LINE SPACING 2
L----!----!----!----!----!----!----!----!----!----!--------R

Fig. 7-3.   Status and ruler line display (typescript)

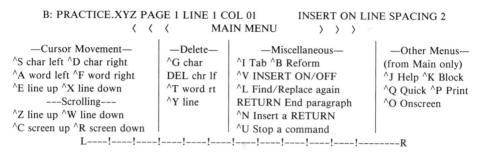

Fig. 7-4. Main Menu, Status Line and Ruler Line as they appear before Help Level is changed.

characters from the left margin, the status line will say "COL 16" because that's where the cursor is located at that moment.

DEFAULT SETTINGS

WordStar has a number of *default* settings. These are things that are in place automatically. When you first load WordStar into your computer, it will be set for: a 65-character-length line, a left margin that's eight characters wide, single-spaced lines, "insert mode" turned on, automatic right-hand justification (ruler-even right side of the typewritten material), automatic page numbering at the bottom of each page, and automatic hyphen-help (we'll get into that later).

You may want to change a few of these things. For example, you may not want those page numbers on the bottom, so the first thing you do at the top of your very first page is type .OP. That is a "dot command" which will not be printed.

Any time a period appears in Column 01, WordStar interprets it as a print command of some kind, and the letters (and numbers) that follow the period tell the program what to do. That .OP means "Omit Page" (number). There are other useful dot commands that we'll get into in the next chapter, but this one is important and should go on the top of *all* of your documents unless you really want that page number neatly centered on the bottom of each page. Sometimes, it does come in handy.

USING THE MAIN MENU

That "Main Menu" contains all of the [Ctl] command functions you'll want to use when entering text. Every one of those little "carets'' (∧) in front of a letter means hold down the **[Ctl]** key while stroking that letter. How to move the cursor around the screen is the first and most important thing you'll want to learn. Many computer keyboards have a set of cursor control keys—four keys with arrows on them—which may or may not work with the WordStar you have installed in your computer.

If the WordStar has been installed and ''patched'' properly, you can use these arrow cursor movement keys. If not, well, WordStar has other ways. Moving the cursor to the left one character (one space) requires a touch of **[Ctl]** S. Moving the cursor to the right one character (one space) requires a touch of **[Ctl]** D. Moving up one line is **[Ctl]** E and moving down one line is **[Ctl]** X. You can't move the cursor down if no lines have already been typed or carriage returns entered below the cursor position. The cursor will not move into unused areas of the screen—areas where you haven't already created some text.

One easy way to remember these key positions: they form a plus sign (+) or cross, and it seems very logical the way it's laid out. If you look at Fig. 7–5, you'll see the key layout used in WordStar and that two additional keys outside the + sign (some people call it a ''diamond'') are the ''A'' and ''F'' keys which also move the cursor. **[Ctl]** A moves the cursor left one *word* and **[Ctl]** F moves the cursor right one *word*.

Fig. 7–5. Six keys for moving the cursor in WordStar files form a cross or ''diamond'' pattern on the keyboard, making it easy to remember which is which.

SCROLLING

The next set of commands has to do with something called *scrolling*. If you think of the screen as a small window that's looking at a long, continuous sheet of paper, you'll have a better idea of what's going on. With scrolling, you're simply moving this "window" up or down on the long sheet or "scroll" of paper.

To scroll up one line (move the window up one line on the text), type **[Ctl]** W. Unfortunately, the perspective is different to different people. The programmers who wrote WordStar call this scrolling *down*. It moves the *text* down, but moves the window, which is seen from your perspective, *up*. To scroll down one line (move text *up*), type **[Ctl]** X. To scroll up one screen or "window" (move the text down 11 lines with the Main Menu in place; 17 lines without the Main Menu), type **[Ctl]** R. To scroll down one screen (move the text *up*), type **[Ctl]** C. These commands give you a lot of flexibility and let you move around the screen very quickly.

DELETING

The delete commands are potentially very dangerous. If you use **[Ctl]** G, you delete the single character directly *at* the cursor. Stroking the DELete key with no **[Ctl]** keystroke deletes the character to the left of the cursor and moves the cursor into the "hole" that this leaves. The text to the right of the cursor will follow, closing up the space.

If you type **[Ctl]** T, this will delete one *word* to the right of the cursor, starting with the character or space at the cursor location. A word ends with a punctuation mark or a space, and this particular delete command can be very handy in *all* of your word processing.

The really dangerous command is **[Ctl]** Y which deletes the entire line that the cursor is on. Be extra careful when using this command, since once the line is deleted, it's lost and gone forever.

This is one of WordStar's bad features. Some word processing programs will "hold" deleted text in a special temporary storage space so you can retrieve anything you delete by mistake. Not so with WordStar, so be extra careful.

A very handy delete command that's not on the Main Menu is **[Ctl]** QY, which will delete the entire line *to the right of the cursor*.

Also note under "Miscellaneous" commands is **[Ctl]** V which turns the *Insert Mode* on and off. This kind of control command is known as a "toggle" because it acts like a toggle switch (like the light switch on the wall) to turn something on or off.

The default version of most WordStar installations has the Insert Mode turned on. This means that anything you type in the middle of a line or word pushes everything else ahead of it like a snowplow. You can then go in after you've finished adding the new material and clean up the remaining text without any danger of losing a lot of valuable material.

With the Insert Mode off, when you type over existing material, the old text is erased while you type. This is especially handy when correcting misspellings with the same number of characters, or correcting a single wrong character. It can definitely save a lot of keystrokes. But for the most part, it's handier to keep the Insert Mode turned on. The status line will say "INSERT ON" or if it's off, it will simply have a blank spot where that statement would normally appear.

OTHER MENUS

The Main Menu lists five other menus, called up with the **[Ctl]** key and the menu letter. These are labeled: ^J (Help); ^Q (Quick); ^K (Block); ^P (Print); and ^O (Onscreen).

Let's look at ^O, the "Onscreen" menu. This contains many of the parameters that you may want to change when you first set up your file, such as margin settings, right justification, hyphen help and line spacing.

When you type **[Ctl]** O and the Onscreen menu appears, you may then type any of the letters that appear on the screen, such as "R" (Right margin) to change a setting. You will then be asked:

RIGHT MARGIN COLUMN NUMBER (ESCAPE for cursor column)?

When you first go into WordStar, your right margin is automatically set for column 65. If you want to change it to 75, simply type **[Ctl]** OP then type 75 **[Return],** and the R on the right side of the ruler line (top of screen) will move to the new location.

Bear in mind that your computer is limited to a screen that's 80 columns wide—for a working line width of 79 columns. You can certainly set wider margins, but they're a royal pain to work with, since you have to scroll horizontally on each line to read what you have. If you want to have text that's 132 columns wide, set your right margin for 66 and then reset it to 132 after you've made all the changes and corrections. A quick touch of the **[Ctl]** B key will reform to the new margin width after everything is in place. If you're setting up a wide chart—well, that's a different matter—and you'll just have to live with the horizontal scrolling. We'll get into reforming and reformatting text later on.

If you want to set a whole bunch of things on the ^O Menu, you don't have to call up the menu each time. Instead, just type **[Ctl]** OJ, for example, to turn Right Justification off. Typing **[Ctl]** OR immediately calls up the right margin reset prompt (question), and **[Ctl]** OH will turn off the hyphen-help toggle. You can even reset the TAB stops with the O-Menu.

THE K-MENU

The K-Menu handles block operations—anything that involves placing markers and moving blocks of material around. This is the "Cut and Paste" menu and the "Save" menu. The most useful single command in this section is **[Ctl]** KD, which saves your open file to the disk, and then gets you out of there back to the No-File Menu.

The second most useful command is **[Ctl]** KS, which saves your file but stays in the file, letting you return to the exact location you were in when you started the save operation. It's important to *do this save frequently,* because the slightest glitch in your electrical power line, or any other disturbance, such as static electricity, can make your computer "forget" all that material in its transient memory (RAM). When this happens, a lot of your work and time go down the drain.

Other things can cause such a disaster. You can jostle a wrong key when you're busy taking some notes on a telephone conversation. Someone can come into your office, and you forget what you were doing and do something accidentally . . . the list goes on.

As a rule of thumb, when you're using WordStar, the *instant* there is an interruption *of any kind*—the phone ringing, someone coming into your office, someone asking you a question—type **[Ctl]** KS. Make this an automatic reflex action, and you'll never be sorry.

Placing Block Markers

The K-Menu's block operations are exciting and enormous time-savers. To begin, you must mark the beginning and end of a block. This can be a sentence, a paragraph, a page, even 10 pages. Place the cursor at the beginning of the block and stroke **[Ctl]** KB (B for the first letter in the word "Block"). The symbol ⟨B⟩ will appear at that point.

Then move the cursor to the end of the block, and stroke **[Ctl]** KK (K is the last letter of the word "BlocK"). One of two things will happen: either a ⟨K⟩ symbol will appear there, or all the copy in the block will suddenly be reversed (black letters on a white or green or amber background). The block is now marked.

You can do any of several things with this block. If you want to move it somewhere else, find the new location, put the cursor there, and then stroke **[Ctl]** KV. This will move the block to the new location.

If you don't want to move it but want *an exact copy of it,* type **[Ctl]** KC at the new location. This is very handy when compiling catalog lists of items from the same source; you only have to keystroke the source vendor's name, address, and phone number once and then copy it as often as needed using the copy block operation.

If you want to delete (erase) the material in the block, stroke **[Ctl]** KY. Careful! Erase it, and it's gone.

You can also take this material and pull it out of the file and put it into a totally separate file with **[Ctl]** KW (W for Write). When you stroke **[Ctl]** KW, the computer will ask you:

NAME OF FILE TO WRITE MARKED TEXT ON?

Answer the question with a *new* filename, followed by a **[Return]**. WordStar will then *copy* the marked block into this new file, but will not do anything to the original marked block in your current file. It's up to you to delete this (**[Ctl]** KY) *after you are absolutely sure that the block has been successfully copied.*

How do you do this? If it's a fairly short block, and your printer isn't being used, you can print it out without exiting from your current file. Again, using the K-Menu, stroke [Ctl] KP (P for Print). This gives you access to the letter commands in the No-File Menu. You will be asked:

NAME OF FILE TO PRINT?

Answer with: NEWFILE.XYZ (the name of the new file into which you wrote the marked block of text) and hit the ESCAPE key. The printer will chatter away immediately and you'll be able to see the text that you had copied into a new file. Once you're satisfied that the block has been successfully written into the new file, you can stroke [Ctl] KY to delete the block in your current file.

A very useful command is [Ctl] KR (Read a file), which will call up any file you name and copy it into your currently open file. This is especially handy for using standing formats, detailed document headings, for writing contracts, and using standing standard (boilerplate) paragraphs or pages as part of a longer document.

THE "HELP" MENU

Typing [Ctl] J calls up the "Help" menu which can change the top-of-screen menu display, and contains a number of explanations about how certain menus and functions actually operate. It's pretty self-explanatory, and it's handy to have around.

The Q Menu (Quick Menu) has a number of useful features. Using [Ctl] Q with other cursor and scrolling control letters will do some very handy things. Type [Ctl] QD, and the cursor moves to the far right of the line. Type [Ctl] QS, and the cursor moves to the far left of the line. If you type [Ctl] QR, you will move to the very beginning of the file, while [Ctl] QC will move you to the end of the file—all in a blink of the eye—unless it's a very long file. Then it may take a few seconds.

The "Find" mode is [Ctl] QF, while "Find and Replace" is started by typing [Ctl] QA. Type [Ctl] QY and you delete everything in the line to the right of the cursor, while if you type [Ctl] Q-DEL (delete key), you will delete the entire line to the left of the cursor.

Getting to the top of the *screen* (not the file) takes a [Ctl] QE and a [Ctl] QX gets you to the bottom of the screen.

You can place index markers from ⟨0⟩ to ⟨9⟩ by typing **[Ctl]** K and the numeral. This will place a numbered marker at the cursor location. These markers don't print, and are not saved when you close the file with a **[Ctl]** KD or a **[Ctl]** KX.

Later, to find marker ⟨1⟩, type **[Ctl]** Q1 and this moves the cursor to text marker ⟨1⟩. You can also move quickly to the beginning or end of a marked block (⟨B⟩ or ⟨K⟩) by typing **[Ctl]** QB or **[Ctl]** QK. With some computers, you must type **[Ctl]** K or **[Ctl]** Q, then *remove* your finger from the control key before typing the following numeral or letter.

The P Menu or "Print" menu is used for setting up such things as margins, justification, line spacing, and so forth, and will be covered in the "Setup" portion of the next chapter. There are certain basic steps to go through with this menu and with entering dot commands when you first load WordStar into your computer. But as long as WordStar remains in the computer's RAM and the computer stays turned on, the special parameters and setups that you select will remain in place—no matter how often you close files and open others.

WordStar is your servant, provided you use it that way, and aren't overawed by the very depth and complexity of the things it's capable of doing. Chances are you'll never use 80 percent of WordStar's capability. But what you can do with that other 20 percent is dynamite!

8
Page Setup and Getting Started

Starting your very first file can be a bit intimidating. If you want to practice a bit, you can copy a sample file that comes with the WordStar disk and play with this until you feel a little more sure of yourself.

Here's the setup:

1. Load WordStar by typing WS **[Return]**
2. Log Disk B by typing L; then B: **[Return]**
3. Copy the file EXAMPLE.TXT by typing the letter O (for cOpy). Answer the first query NAME OF FILE TO COPY FROM? with:

A:EXAMPLE.TXT **[Return]**

The computer will then ask:

NAME OF FILE TO COPY TO?

Answer this with some inconsequential file name such as:

PRACTICE **[Return]**

Once this copy operation is completed, you will have a file named "PRACTICE" on Disk B and you can open it and edit it to your heart's content without any fear of disturbing the original file.

LOGGED AND NON-LOGGED DISK DRIVES

Note that when you called up the original file, you used an A: in front of the file name. This tells the computer to look for the file on Disk A, since you are logged into Disk B. Also, because you're already logged into Disk B, you don't need to put a B: in front of the new file name. The computer *automatically assumes* that you want the logged disk drive when you don't put a disk drive letter in front of the file name.

Now let's work on that example copy that came with the WordStar disk. It starts with a commercial called, "^S^B OVERVIEW of WordStar^S^B".

It's set up to use the *default* settings such as: 65-character-wide line, right-hand justification, and single-spacing. It may not look right; the right margin doesn't appear to be justified, and that's because the text includes a number of print control functions such as ^S (underscore) and ^B (boldface). These are actually special *toggles* since they turn functions on and off like a toggle (wall) switch (see Fig. 8–1).

You get these by typing [Ctl] PS and [Ctl] PB which appears on the text line at ^S and ^B. These symbols and letters *do not print on the printer*. Instead, they tell the printer to underscore everything that follows the ^S until it encounters another ^S. The same is true of the ^B—it tells the printer to **boldface** everything between the ^B symbols by typing over twice.

If you want to see the actual layout of the text without all those distracting markers in place, type [Ctl] OD (Omit Display), and the markers will disappear and you'll see that text nicely centered and right-justified. To put the markers back on, type [Ctl] OD once again (see Fig. 8–2).

Once you have the PRACTICE file loaded and in place, play around with the cursor movements. You'll see how easy it really is to use the [Ctl] key with the keyboard to move the cursor around. After about two weeks of actually working with WordStar, you'll be able to get along without the Main Menu, and this will give you a larger screen area with which to work.

To get rid of the Main Menu, Type [Ctl] J, then type H2. This will still display all the additional menus when you call them up, but will give you a full screen to work with when you're doing text entry

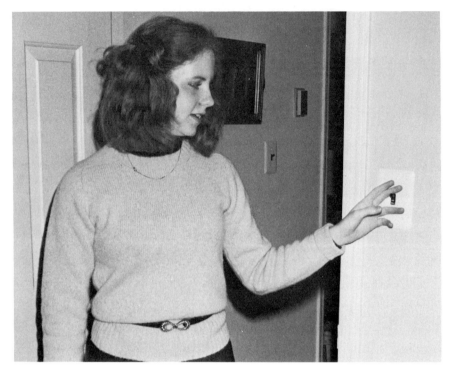

Fig. 8-1.   Just like a wall toggle switch, a computer command toggle turns a function on or off.

and editing. If someone else who needs that Main Menu takes over the computer, you can get it back with **[Ctl]** J, and then H3.

OPENING A NEW FILE

Once you've had enough "Practice," try opening a file of your own. Let's say you want to write a letter to International Tabasco Sauce Co., and you want it to be one page long. The first thing to do is to decide on a name for the file. It could simply be TABLET01.915. Here's how we decided on that name: TAB for Tabasco, LET for letter, 01 to indicate that it's the first letter in the Tabasco letter file, and the extension of 915 to indicate the date (September 15). Remember, you can use up to eight characters for a FILENAME and up to three characters for an EXTENSION or FILETYPE, following

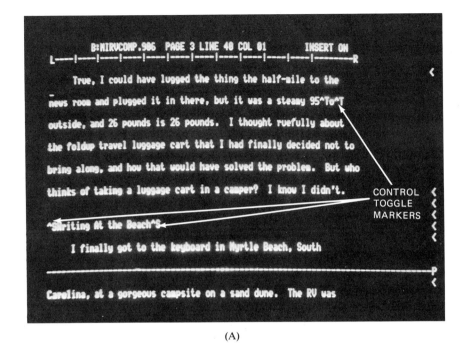

(A)

Fig. 8-2. WordStar lets you see print commands that are embedded in the text (A), but if you have trouble visualizing the actual line layout, you can turn these markers off (B). Turning them off doesn't erase them; they're still in the text file right where you left them.

a period. The three-character extension is optional, but most people find it very useful.

Starting From No-File Menu

To start from the No-File Menu, type the letter "D", and you will be asked:

NAME OF FILE TO EDIT?

Answer with:

TABLET01.915 **[Return]**

The computer will display the legend: NEW FILE and in a moment

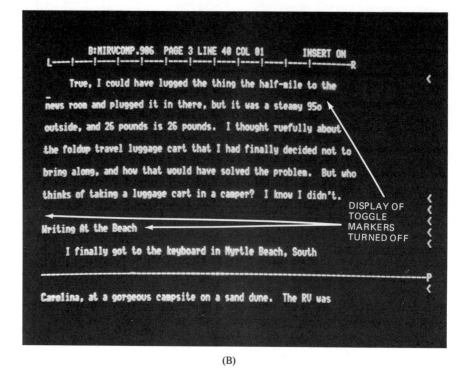

B:NIRVCOMP.986 PAGE 3 LINE 40 COL 01   INSERT ON

True, I could have lugged the thing the half-mile to the

news room and plugged it in there, but it was a steamy 95o

outside, and 26 pounds is 26 pounds. I thought ruefully about

the foldup travel luggage cart that I had finally decided not to

bring along, and how that would have solved the problem. But who

thinks of taking a luggage cart in a camper? I know I didn't.

DISPLAY OF
TOGGLE
Writing At the Beach   MARKERS
TURNED OFF

I finally got to the keyboard in Myrtle Beach, South

Carolina, at a gorgeous campsite on a sand dune. The RV was

(B)

Fig. 8-2 (B).   Screen display showing toggle markers that appear in Fig. 8-2 (A) turned off. The toggle markers are still embedded in the file, but are not displayed.

you'll get the status line, Main Menu and ruler line at the top portion of the screen. The status line will display at the far left, the filename: B:TABLET01.915.

The cursor will be blinking in position at line 1, column 1, and in this location, type;

.OP

This will Omit Page numbers. It's a one-page letter, and you don't want a neat number 1 on the bottom of the page, do you?

Let's assume that you do not want right-hand justification, and don't want to play around with hyphens. So type [Ctl] OJ and then [Ctl] OH.

Let's also assume that you want the line width to be 70 characters instead of the default's 65. So type **[Ctl]** OR, and then type 70 **[Return]**. The line width will be reset.

If you're using a 12-pitch (elite) print wheel in your printer, on the line just under that .OP, type **[Ctl]** PA. This will plug ^A into the first two columns of that line. This means "Alternate" pitch, since most Daisy-wheel printers have a default mode of 10 pitch. With some printers, you may not need this ^A, but it won't hurt anything if you put it in.

If you want to set the TAB stops, you can do this, too. The default settings are at every five spaces up to column 55. They are the ! marks on the ruler line at the top of the page on the screen. First, clear all the TAB stops by typing **[Ctl]** ON, then the letter A (for "all") and **[Return]**. All the ! marks will disappear.

We find that the most convenient TAB stops for general correspondence and manuscript work are at columns 6 and 41. Type **[Ctl]** OI to set a **TAB** stop. The computer will say:

SET TAB AT COLUMN (ESCAPE for cursor column)?

Type the number 6 **[Return]**. A ! will now appear on the ruler at column 6. Do it over: **[Ctl]** OI, and this time type 41 **[Return]**. A ! symbol will appear at column 41. This is a good location for typing the date, close, and signature line—all nicely lined up in the same column.

THOSE RIGHT-HAND SYMBOLS

During the course of typing, *do not* use the **[Return]** key at all except at the end of a paragraph. If you look at the right of the screen, you'll see a string of periods (.) down the right side. These are lines that are totally blank and are not in your file in any way. When you type and reach the end of a line, keep typing. The automatic *word wrap* will take over and will move the overlapping word to the next line and the period in the right column will disappear. WordStar has just generated a *soft carriage return* on that line.

When you hit **[Return]** key, a ⟨ symbol will appear in the rightmost column of the screen. This is a *hard carriage return*. You'll need two of them so hit **[Return]** twice at the end of each paragraph in a single-spaced letter. You can indent the beginning of the paragraph with the TAB key or leave it flush left—whatever your office letter-writing style happens to be.

Another symbol that appears in the rightmost column is a plus sign (+), which means that there is more text on that line that is too long for the screen to display (see Fig. 8-3). The automatic word wrap doesn't show on the screen if you have line lengths that are more than 79 characters. You will then get a lot of plus signs (+) in column 80.

If you want to scroll horizontally to see this material, simply type **[Ctl]** F several times and you'll get to see the rest of the line. To return to the left and the principal screen display, type **[Ctl]** X, and this will get the cursor to column 1 on the next line.

When you use the "line overstrike" control (**[Ctl]** PM), a minus sign (−) will appear in column 80 (see Fig. 8-3). This means that the line that follows will print directly over the line that has the − sign at the right. This is useful for underscoring strings of words— especially if you want the *spaces* underscored as well. Using the underscore toggle (**[Ctl]** PS) will only underscore printed characters— not the spaces in between.

To use the toggle to underscore spaces, you'd have to type something like this:

^SNow_is_the_time_for_all_good_men_to_leave.^S

That's a lot of extra work to get all those spaces underscored. Instead type this:

Now is the time for all good men to leave. **[Ctl]** PM

You'll get a − sign in column 80 and the cursor will move down one line. Line up the cursor under the N in Now, and holding the shift key down, press the underscore/hyphen key—holding it down so it repeats—just as you would with a conventional IBM typewriter. When the underscore has reached the space below the period, stop. Then hit the **[Return]** key and continue by typing your next line.

The remarkable feature of WordStar is that it shows you almost *exactly* what you're going to get on your printed copy—spacing and all—but to use this feature, you have to follow the rules that are built into the WordStar program.

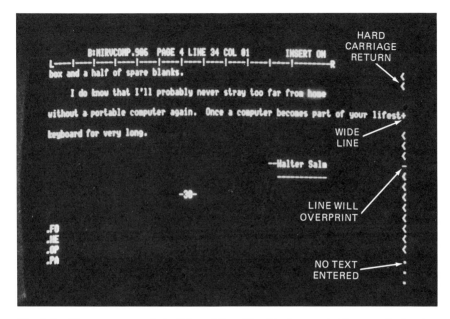

Fig. 8-3.   Those strange marks in Column 80 are WordStar's way of telling you what's going on in each line. The < symbol means a hard carriage return; the plus (+) sign means that the line extends beyond the screen width; a minus (−) sign means that the next line will overprint the existing line, and a period (.) means that nothing has been entered on that line.

Remember, if there are a number of ^S and ^B and other control toggles in the text, it will look a little strange, and some of the lines will look too long because those control symbols each occupy space on the screen. If you want to view it in its correct spacing, simply turn off the markers with **[Ctl] OD**. The toggle markers stay in the file, but since they themselves don't print out, they are hidden from your view—which many people find much more comfortable.

SINGLE-PAGE LETTER FORMAT

Now here's the drill for setting up a single-spaced single-page letter with 12-pitch type (for 10-pitch, omit **[Ctl] PA [Return]**):

In No-File Menu, type letter D. Type file name and **[Return]**.

When the new file has opened, do this:
Type .OP **[Return]**
Type **[Ctl]** PA **[Return]**
Type **[Ctl]** OJ
Type **[Ctl]** OH
Type **[Ctl]** ON
Type A **[Return]**
Type **[Ctl]** OI
Type 6 **[Return]**
Type **[Ctl]** OI
Type 41 **[Return]**

Now you're ready to start typing.

One other thing; if you're using a letterhead, you'll have to experiment to see how many hard carriage returns it will take to give you the proper spacing from the top of the page to the date. Don't be dismayed if the letter doesn't come out looking just right. A few keystrokes will correct it, and your printer will do all the retyping for you.

MULTIPLE PAGES

If you want to type a document of more than one page, WordStar makes it relatively easy to plug in such neat things as running page headers, page numbers *where you want them,* page footers, and so on. To do these, you use those good old Dot Commands. The dot commands in these cases work like toggles; you have to turn them off at the end of the document, or WordStar will print additional pages with headers and footers on blank sheets.

Here's how to set them up. First, for footlines that are below the bottom margin of your typewritten page, bring you cursor down to the bottom of the page—just above that dashed line with the letter "P" at the right. That dashed line indicates the bottom of the printed portion of your page. Suppose you want to type: "(Continued on next page)" centered on the bottom of each page. Type: (Continued on next page), then type **[Ctl]** OC. This will center the text automatically.

Next, type **[Ctl]** QS. This will move the cursor to column 1 of that same line. Now type: .FO. The page break line will immediately move down one line to make room for this statement, and the phrase "(Continued on next page)" will appear centered on the bottom of *every page* until you put in another .FO with the period in column 1. You can just type .FO with nothing after it, and this will turn off the footing command on the last page.

Now suppose you want a header with running page numbers at the top of each page. Go to the top of page 2, hit **[Return]** once or twice to give you a little room, and move the cursor to line 1, column 1 of that page. Type .HE (for HEading). Move the cursor across to about mid-page (TAB to 41 if that's convenient) and type your header, such as:

.HE   Special Report on XYZ Company

Follow it with − Page # − like this:

.HE   Special Report on XYZ Company − Page # −

On page 2 and every page that follows, WordStar will replace the # sign with the proper page number. You can use this same # for page numbering with the .FO if you want the page numbers in the footlines.

As with the .FO, you must turn off the header feature at the end of your document by typing .HE with the period in column 1 and a blank line to the right of the .HE.

A convenient way of setting up this whole thing is to go to the end of the document and type the following *after* the end of your text:

.FO   (Continued on the next page)   ⟨

                                                        ⟨

.HE   Special Report on the XYZ Company − Page # −   ⟨

Then put block markers around it so it will look something like this:

⟨B⟩
.FO ˈ (Continued on the next page) ⟨
  ⟨
.HE Special Report on the XYZ Company — Page # — ⟨
⟨K⟩

Now all you have to do is to backspace to the point where the page break is displayed between pages 1 and 2, put your cursor right above the page break line, and type **[Ctl]** KV. The entire block will move into place and will give you just the right amount of top and bottom margin spacing.

The actual ending of the document should look something like this:

text text text text text text text text text text text text text
text text text text text text. ⟨
  ⟨
* * * ⟨
.FO ⟨
.HE ⟨
  ⟨
.PA ⟨

That .PA at the end indicates the end of the page and will presumably stop the printer. A page break line may or may not appear just below it. If the page break line does appear, make sure there are no hard carriage returns below it (⟨), or the printer will try to print another page for you. If there are such hard carriage returns, you can get rid of them easily by putting the cursor just to the right of the .PA and typing **[Ctl]** T a few times.

THE BIG QUESTION MARK

One other symbol that can appear in the rightmost column (column 80) is a question mark (?), and this happens when you type a period in column 1, with nothing after it. The ? is telling you that you haven't entered a *complete* dot command. Sometimes a warning flag will appear, such as:

PUT AT FILE BEGINNING FOR CORRECT PAGE BREAK DIS-
PLAY

This happens with such commands as .MT (Margin Top) when it
appears after other dot commands. Suppose you want a deeper top
margin on your page. Your first line should say: .MT 6 (or however
many additional lines you want the top margin to have). You can
actually start off your document with a whole array of dot commands, one right above the other. These commands *do not occupy
printed lines of space,* and if you look at the line number display in
the status lines, you'll see that after typing three or four lines of dot
commands, you're still on line 1.

The computer will not print anything that's on the line after a dot
command, unless it's a command such as .FO or .HE. It regards any
other such material as a comment. So be careful that you don't try
to crowd some text onto the same line as a dot command. This can
be very frustrating and confusing when it comes time to print out
the document.

One other thing; since any period in column 1 will be interpreted
by WordStar as the beginning of a dot command, be careful of such
literary devices as ". . ." which might put a period there during text
reformatting. This can cause trouble. If you absolutely *must* print a
period in column 1, you can "fool" WordStar by typing a pair of
control symbol toggles at the beginning of that line like this:

^S^S. . .

You have occupied column 1 with a control toggle, which you have
then immediately turned off. You'll get that period printed in column 1 with no further questions asked.

9
Quick Setup and Perfecting Your Style

Any typist or secretary must do some basic setup on a typewriter before typing a letter, report, manuscript, or whatever. The typist must set margins, replace the type ball element if necessary, select the proper type pitch, set spacing and TAB stops. The same is true with WordStar, but a few additional settings have to be added because of the "Default" settings that are already set in the program.

WHAT'S A DEFAULT?

A default setting is simply the set of parameters—margins, spacing, TAB stops, etc., that are in place when you first load WordStar into your computer. These settings are on the original program disk and follow you into each copy you make. It's up to you, after you load WordStar, to make changes so these things meet your own needs for a particular typing job. It's not a big deal.

Here's what you get with the initial default that comes with WordStar:

1. Single spacing
2. 10-pitch type (10 characters to the inch)
3. 65-character-wide line
4. 55 *typewritten* lines per page
5. 3/4-inch margins—top, bottom, left, and right
6. Right-hand justification
7. 11 TAB stops set at 5-character intervals

8. INSERT mode turned on
9. Automatic page numbering—middle bottom of each page
10. Hyphen-help turned on
11. Automatic word wrap
12. Ruler line at top of text display
13. Page break display
14. Status line at top of screen
15. Main Menu displayed between status line and ruler line

We're going to take a look at each of these defaults and show you how to change them to suit your own needs.

Single-Spacing

WordStar gives you the option of single-spacing or putting as many as eight spaces between lines. If you type **[Ctl]** OS, this prompt (question) will appear above the ruler line:

ENTER space OR NEW LINE SPACING (1–9):

If you're in the default condition of single-spacing, there will be a blank area at the right end of the status line. If you enter the number "2" in response to the prompt, the phrase:

LINE SPACING 2

will appear at the right of the status line. If you hit the space bar, it will simply turn off the prompt and return you to your previous line spacing situation. Hitting the **[Return]** will do the same thing.

Changing Type Pitch

The type pitch is probably one of the least understood characteristics of any word processing program and printer. Some printers are totally software-controlled. That is, you adjust the type pitch *from the computer* with your word processing program indicators or control symbols. Other printers have a switch selector that *you must use* no matter what control characters you put into your word processing file. The Diablo 630 is an example of a software-controlled pitch printer. The Daisywriter is typical of the type on which you *must* change a printer control selector.

Whichever way it works, you also have to remember to put in a type wheel that is appropriate for the particular pitch you're using. If you use a 10-pitch wheel (also known as "pica," or 10 characters per inch) and set your printer for 12-pitch, the letters will be cramped and crowded together. If you use a 12-pitch wheel (also known as "elite," or 12 characters per inch) and run the printer at 10-pitch, the printing will look too strung out and will have an odd looking amount of space between each character.

Most printers will also provide 15-pitch as well, and this requires a very special type wheel. Typically, this is used for creating address labels and some types of bookkeeping and billing forms. The type faces that are available in this size are very stylized and simple— something like the type that's used in the telephone directory. It's not something you'd ordinarily use for correspondence, reports, etc.

Right Justification

The decision to justify the right side of the page (ruler-straight type) or to have ragged right is a matter of individual choice. While it may look nice, unless your printer and typewheel provide proportional characters and microspacing, it may look rather strange. This is because WordStar performs the justification by placing extra spaces in between words in lines that otherwise don't come out even. See Fig. 9–1 for an example of single-spaced, right-justified type.

The nice thing about right-hand justification is that WordStar makes it so darned easy, you can try it both ways and then decide which you want to use.

Line Width

The ruler line at the top of your screen working area shows the actual width of the printed line (see Fig. 9–2). The left margin is marked with an "L" and the right margin is marked with an "R". The exclamation points (!) are the TAB stops.

To change the right margin settings, type [Ctl] OR. The computer will ask:

The   decision to justify the right side of the page (ruler-
straight type) or to have ragged right is a matter of individual
choice.   While it may look nice, unless your printer and
typewheel provide proportional characters and microspacing, it
may look rather strange.   This is because the justification   is
performed   by WordStar by placing lots of extra spaces in between
words in lines that otherwise don't come out even.

The decision to justify the right side of the page (ruler-
straight type) or to have ragged right is a matter of individual
choice.   While it may look nice, unless your printer and
typewheel provide proportional characters and microspacing, it
may look rather strange.   This is because the justification is
performed by WordStar by placing lots of extra spaces in between
words in lines that otherwise don't come out even.

Fig. 9-1.   Can't decide whether you want right-justified or ragged right printout of your materials? WordStar lets you see it and print it out both ways and you can take your pick.

RIGHT MARGIN COLUMN NUMBER (ESCAPE for cursor column)?

If you want to reset the line width to 79 characters (the maximum
you can get on an 80-column screen without running off the page
and generating a "+" sign in column 80), type the number 79 **[Return]**. Unlike the line spacing question and answer, for setting mar-

```
     B:FILENAME.EXT   PAGE 1 LINE 14 COL Ø1             INSERT ON  LINE SPACING 2
L----!----!----!----!----!----!----!----!----!----!----!-------R
.OP
```

The "No-File" menu comes up automatically as the second screen
(after displaying the copyright notice and equipment installation
list) when you invoke WordStar with the "WS" command. Typing any
letter on this menu will start a WordStar operation. The cursor
blinks to the right of the "S Run SpellStar" command.

    If you invoke MailMerge or SpellStar without actually having
those programs installed on the program disk, an error message
will be displayed, and you must type the "Escape" key to get back
to the command mode in the No-File Menu.

    The most common command to use at this point is "D" -- to
reopen or start a document file.
[ ]

Fig. 9-2.   A 25-line screen shrinks to 23 lines when you have status and ruler lines at the top.
The WordStar status line tells you which disk drive you're using (B:), the filename, page
number, line number, column, insert on (if it's on) and line spacing (if it's other than single-
spacing). The ruler line shows you margin locations and tab stops.

gins, you *must* hit the **[Return]** key after typing in the number. The reason: line spacing requires a one-digit answer; margin setup can be one, two or three digits, and the **[Return]** key is the only way we can tell the computer when we're ready to enter this choice.

WordStar automatically gives you eight columns of white space for a left margin *all the time.* That left margin setting on the screen (the "L" on the ruler line—see Fig. 9-2) is the left end of the *printed line.* If you want to move the typewritten material closer to the left side of the page you can do one of two things: move the location of the paper in the printer, or insert a dot command: .PO 2 (Page Offset, 2 spaces) which will give you spacing of just two character widths from the left edge of the paper.

This particular dot command can be inserted in the middle of a page of text if you desire—and can be used like a toggle. If you have a few lines of text that you want to extend out into the margin, put .PO 2 on the line before this material. You can restore the normal margin width right after this typed material with a .PO 8.

This can also work in reverse. If you want a block of material to be indented without having to go through the work of tabbing all of it to the proper column, add the number of columns to 8. If, for example, you want a block of material to start on column 10, add 10 to 8 and type .PO 18 just before the block you want to be typed this way. At the end of this material, simply restore the "normal" paper margin with .PO 8 with the period in column 1 on the screen.

Fig. 9-3 shows how it will look on the screen.

Fig. 9-4 shows how this same material will actually print out.

Try to get accustomed to using these dot commands; they can make your life a lot easier. Here's another shortcut using the page offset command; it's called *addressing envelopes.*

Assume you've just typed a letter like the one shown in Fig. 9-5.

Now, let's prepare an envelope. First, make sure you end the letter with a .PA with the period in column 1.

Now go back and mark the address section in the letter with block markers as shown in Fig. 9-6.

Then inset about 10 hard carriage returns to get the approximate location for the envelope on the next "page" on your computer screen.

Now copy the address at the envelope location with a **[Ctl]** KC.

*   *   *

Here are the key specifications for the typical business

computer:

```
.PO 18                                                      <
-Built-in monitor screen                                    <
-Two disk drives                                            <
-Full typewriter keyboard with separate number keypad       <
-User memory (RAM) of 64K minimum                           <
-Z-80A or 8080 microprocessor                               <
-CP/M-compatible operating system                           <
-Serial and/or parallel input/output ports                  <
.PO 8                                                       <
```

All of these parameters should be part of the basic computer

system.   Adding a printer and other peripherals can just add to

its flexibility.

Fig. 9–3.   Typing .PO 18 before a block of text will indent it 10 columns from the left margin. To reset the normal left margin, insert .PO 8 to get back to the normal "default" left margin.

*   *   *

Here are the key specifications for the typical business

computer:

```
              -Built-in monitor screen
              -Two disk drives
              -Full typewriter keyboard with separate number keypad
              -User memory (RAM) of 64K minimum
              -Z-80A or 8080 microprocessor
              -CP/M-compatible operating system
              -Serial and/or parallel input/output ports
```

All of these parameters should be part of the basic computer

system.   Adding a printer and other peripherals can just add to

its flexibility.

Fig. 9–4.   Using the .PO commands shown in Fig. 9–3 will give you a printout that looks like this.

*   *   *

```
.OP                                                              <
                                                                 <
                                                                 <
                                          April 17, 1985         <
                                                                 <
Mr. Gerald Kasser, President                                     <
CableCast of Scranton                                            <
375 E. Railroad Avenue                                           <
Scranton, PA 14105                                               <
                                                                 <
Dear Mr. Kasser:                                                 <
                                                                 <
```

We appreciate your recent letter and order for two new color
cameras and are shipping the hardware to your studio this week.

We think that you will find our cameras are not only on the
leading edge of today's technology, but they will also outperform
any equipment you have previously used, with higher reliability,
easier operator setup, and at lower light levels.

You will no doubt be especially pleased with the new low-noise
amplifier circuits that have been miniaturized and share an
integrated circuit chip with the video output amplifier drivers.

One of our customer service engineers will call your studio in a
few days to set up an appointment for installing the cameras and
at that time will provide your technical staff with some on-site
instruction.

Thank you for your order, and we hope to continue our excellent
working relationship.

```
                                          Sincerely,


                                          Robert Weems
                                          Product Service Manager
RW:ea
.PA
```

Fig. 9-5. Typical letter layout.

Move the cursor up one line and type .PO 40. Next, move the cursor
to the line *below* the address. You'll have to insert a hard carriage
return at the end of the address to do this. Now type .PO 8 to restore
the proper margin offset—assuming you have other documents in
the same file. If the envelope is the last page of the file, you don't
have to bother with the .PO 8. Now place a .PA below this to end
the page. This will tell the printer to roll the finished envelope out,

*   *   *

```
                                                        <
<B>                                                     <
Mr. Gerald Kasser, President                            <
CableCast of Scranton                                   <
375 E. Railroad Avenue                                  <
Scranton, PA 14105                                      <
<K>                                                     <
Dear Mr. Kasser:                                        <
                                                        <
```
We appreciate your recent letter and order for two new color
cameras and are shipping the hardware to your studio this week.

Fig. 9-6.   The letter shown in Fig. 9-5 with block markers surrounding the address section of the letter.

which makes your life just a little easier. The envelope's page should look like Fig. 9-7 on the computer screen.

How Many Lines?

Those nice, neat, top and bottom margins mean a default printout of 55 lines (28 lines of type and 27 spaces for double-spacing), which translates into an attractive looking page if you're using 12-pitch type; for 10-pitch, it might be a bit crowded, and some people prefer to put an .MT 6 at the top of the file. This adds 2 lines of space to the top of the page and gives you 52 lines of printed text per page. That means for double-spacing, you have 25 typed lines and 27 spaces.

TAB Stops

When you first load WordStar, there are 11 TAB stops with five characters of spacing between them. If you want to specify actual locations, they are at columns 6, 11, 16, etc. and are marked by the ! symbols on the ruler line at the top of your text.

If you want to reset the TABs, the easiest thing to do is type **[Ctl]** ON. The computer will then ask you:

CLEAR TAB AT COL (ESCAPE for cursor col; A for all)?

The question is fairly obvious. The easiest thing to do is type "A"

*   *   *


```
.PA
-----------------------------------------------------------------P
                                                                 <
                                                                 <
                                                                 <
                                                                 <
                                                                 <
                                                                 <
                                                                 <
                                                                 <
                                                                 <
                                                                 <
                                                                 <
                                                                 <
.PO 48                                                           <
Mr. Gerald Kasser, President                                     <
CableCast of Scranton                                            <
375 E. Railroad Avenue                                           <
Scranton, PA 14105                                               <
.PO 8                                                            <
.PA                                                              <
-----------------------------------------------------------------P
```

Fig. 9-7. Setting up the envelope with the .PO commands and copying the address from the letter will give a result like this on the screen.

[Return]. All the ! marks will disappear and you have *no* TAB stops. Now set two or three that you really want, such as 6, 11, and 41, which are probably the most useful for general-purpose use.

Do this by typing **[Ctl]** OI. The computer will then ask:

SET TAB AT COLUMN (ESCAPE for cursor column)?

Answer by typing "6" **[Return],** and you'll get a ! at column 6. Repeat the operation for 11 and 41 and you'll be all set.

If you're setting up a chart and want to set the TAB stops on particular column headings as you type them, type your column heading, then move the cursor to the beginning of the word (**[Ctl]** A) and then do this sequence: **[Ctl]** OI, then hit the ESCAPE key. This will set the TAB (!) at the beginning of the column on the chart or tabular matter that you're preparing. It's a quick and easy way to do it.

Then advance to the next position by first typing **[Ctl]** F to move the cursor to the right of the column heading word and then use the space bar to move to the next heading position. An alternative way is to wait until you have all the column headings typed and then use the cursor control keys to find the beginning of each column, and then set each TAB with the ESCAPE key. You may find it to be faster and easier.

INSERT Mode

Many word processor programs normally work with the INSERT mode turned off. They're not designed for continuous insertion, and will accept only a limited amount of inserted material. WordStar can operate either way, and the default condition for most computers has the INSERT turned on. You'll see "INSERT ON" near the right of the status line at the very top of the screen.

With INSERT turned on, everything you type will push anything to the right in front of it like a snowplow, and will not delete anything unless you type specific delete function keys (**[Ctl]** G, **[Ctl]** T, **[Ctl]** Y, DEL, **[Ctl]** QY and **[Ctl]** Q-DEL).

You can turn the INSERT off with a simple toggle command: **[Ctl]** V. This will also turn INSERT back on when it's off. With INSERT off, anything that's in the way will be erased as you type over it. This can be very handy if you want to change lowercase to all CAPS or change some figures that are wrong. The old, incorrect text gives you a template for typing and spacing the new material properly.

But to be on the safe side, it's a good idea to keep the INSERT turned on most of the time. You can always erase (or delete) unwanted material after you finish typing in the new material. This is a very personal decision; it's up to you to decide how many keystrokes are involved in a particular correction with INSERT turned on and with INSERT turned off, and which one you find easier and more convenient to use.

Page Numbering

The normal default for WordStar is to place a nice, neat number in the middle of the bottom margin of each and every page. If you don't like this arrangement, the first thing you do when you open a document file is type .OP in the left upper margin. OP means "Omit Page (number)" and *must* be in place—even on single-page letters. Otherwise, even your nice, neat one-page word-processor-produced letters will have a neat little number 1 in the middle of the bottom margin. You probably don't want this.

You can select and set up other page-numbering routines very easily with WordStar. WordStar lets you make the page number part of a tailor-made header or footline starting with any page you like, and continuing the page numbers, or using any kind of numbering routine you want. Here's how to do it.

Remember those nice footing and header dot commands we described in the previous chapter? Let's take another look at those.

The .FO (Footing) command goes at the bottom of your text page. Here is one way of doing it:

.FO   - Page # -

When you use the number symbol (#), WordStar will paginate correctly, starting with the page where the .FO command appears, replacing the # symbol with the correct page number. If you have used the .OP at the beginning of the file, and do not use a # symbol in a header or a footer, there will be no page numbering. You *only have to type this once.* WordStar will then very nicely print that - Page #- on the bottom of every page that follows.

The same thing is true of headers. By typing .HE (Header or Heading), you can plug in the page number and any special header you like by using the # sign. It will look like this:

.HE   XYZ TRANSCOM INTERNATIONAL -Page # -

This should be at the top of the page—usually page 2, and once again the # will be replaced by the correct page number on the top of each and every page. You only have to type the .HE line once. WordStar will do the rest.

This works fine if the page numbers correspond to the page number that appears on the status line at the top of the screen. But very often, you may have a title page, a covering letter, a summary, or something else that precedes the page-numbered text, and this will throw off your page number sequence so they don't correspond with the page numbers in your file status line. Suppose you start on the first page of your report, but the status line says PAGE 7. You could be in trouble. Because in this case, a .HE command at the top of the second page of your report will make it read - Page 8 - instead of -Page 2 - and so on.

There's a simple remedy for this. It's another dot command. On the top of the page that you want to start renumbering, enter this command: .PN 2 (Page number 2) or .PN 1, or whatever. This command should be *on the first line of your page* and the line below it will contain the .HE command. It will look like this:

.PN 2
.HE   XYZ TRANSCOM INTERNATIONAL - Page # -

Now, the second page of your report will carry the header with the proper page number, and each page that follows it will be properly numbered in sequence. By the way, you don't have to number the pages. You can still use .FO and .HE to set up running footers and headers without page numbers, simply by leaving that # out of the statement.

There's one fly in this utopian ointment, however. WordStar has a built-in glitch (problem) with these commands when it comes time to print out the file. If you want to print out a *specific page* rather than the entire file, you'll have to instruct WordStar to print the *renumbered* page when you tell it what to print—*not* the page number as it appears on the status line.

Since there will be more than one page that's called PAGE 2, for example, WordStar can get confused and you can have a problem printing out the first part of the file.

An easy way to handle this is simply to copy this first section into another, separate file, and print from that. You can do this by placing your block markers (**[Ctl]** KB and **[Ctl]** KK) around the *entire file section*—however many pages long it is, and then typing **[Ctl]** KW to write it all to another file. Then name a new file, hit **[Return],** and voilà! You have a copy of that section in its own, neat separate file. And you can print that file without even leaving the file you have open by typing **[Ctl]** KP and then naming that other file.

If you use **[Ctl]** KP, and you elect to use **[Return]** rather than ESCAPE to execute the print operation, be very careful that you don't type **[Return]** any more times than you need to answer the print control prompts. Otherwise, you'll put a lot of extra, unwanted hard carriage returns in the file you're working on, and you'll end up wondering where they came from later on.

Word Wrap

Word Wrap is an automatic function that takes a little getting used to at first. When you reach the end of a line, *do not* type the **[Return]** key, but just keep on typing. The WordStar program will automatically insert a *soft carriage return*—which shows up as a totally blank space in column 80. The next word will automatically move to the beginning of the next line.

Until you get used to this feature, you'll probably pause at the end of each line and think to yourself, "Now what was it I was supposed to do here?" Answer: just keep typing and forget the **[Return]** key. Once you get accustomed to using this feature, you'll find that it's a big time-saver and your typing speed will increase. The only time you should use the **[Return]** key is when you reach the end of a paragraph.

If you decide, in your great wisdom, that you don't want the word wrap on, you can turn it off with a simple toggle—**[Ctl]** OW. But for now, leave it on. It really is a big help.

Reformatting

Before getting into the rest of the defaults and what to do about them, it's important to understand page reformatting, and how it works.

The basic control for this is **[Ctl]** B. If you've made some changes—additions, deletions, etc. in a paragraph of text, it will look pretty ragged on the screen, and in fact, that's the way it will print. By placing the cursor at the beginning of a paragraph and using the **[Ctl]** B, you can instantly reformat the paragraph. Lines will fill out and break in the proper places, and everything looks great!

Or does it? The reformat key will work down through the text in a blink, but will stop when it reaches a hard carriage return or a word that looks too long and should be hyphenated. The operation will stop, and a long word will hang over the end of the line with the cursor blinking in the middle of it. The computer is asking you if you want to hyphenate that word.

If you don't want a hyphen, just hit **[Ctl]** B again, and the reformatting operation will continue. If you do want a hyphen, move the cursor to the location in the word where you want it and hit the hyphen key (see Fig. 9–8).

In general, hyphen-help is more trouble than it's worth—especially if the text is going to go through any further revisions. If this is the case, you can avoid doing any hyphenation at all by simply turning the hyphen-help toggle off. Do this by typing **[Ctl]** OH when you set up your first WordStar file for the day. With hyphen-help turned off, each **[Ctl]** B will take you through an entire paragraph. Starting the next paragraph will take *two* strokes of **[Ctl]** B—one to get past the hard carriage return at the end of the paragraph, and the next to start the reformatting operation for the next paragraph.

Ruler Line

The ruler line at the top of your text display shows you two things: your left and right margin locations and the TAB stops. You don't absolutely have to have it turned on, but it's there, and it's rather handy to have.

If you want it off, like so many other features, it's toggle-controlled, and a **[Ctl]** OT will make it invisible and give you one extra line of page display on the screen. But it *is* rather comforting to have there—giving you instant information about your margins and TAB stops. It's mostly a matter of taste and how much you feel you need that security blanket.

*   *   *

```
        The   decision  to justify  the right side  of the page   (ruler-
straight  type)  or to  have  ragged right  is a matter  of   individual
choice.   While   it   may   look   nice,   unless   your   printer   and
typewheel   provide  proportional  characters  and   microspacing,   it
may   look  rather  strange.    This  is because  the justification   is
performed   by WordStar  by placing  lots of extra  spaces  in between
words  in lines  that  otherwise  don't come  out even.
```

Fig. 9–8. Reformatting with the justification toggle turned on can take ragged right text and convert it to even block copy like this.

Page Break Display

WordStar will automatically show you the page break with a dashed line followed by the letter ''P.'' It looks like this:

--P

The only problem with this display is that it pops up at the wrong times and places—usually when you're trying to squeeze just one more line on a page. Generally, in the default situation, the page break shows up after 55 lines of *text* or *text and spaces combined*.

You can turn it off with a simple toggle command: **[Ctl]** OP (Omit Page break). But then, your word processing is like working in the dark. You really have to know where that page break comes, even if—and especially if—you don't like the location.

The actual position of the page break display depends on the page length. Normal page length is 66 lines—55 lines of text, 3 lines top margin, 8 lines bottom margin. If you want to type a legal size sheet (8 1/2 × 14), type in a dot command at the top of the file: .PL 86 (Page Length—86 lines). This will move the page break display down 20 lines, giving you 75 lines of text and spacing with the usual margins.

The page break display will move down when you type the .FO command for a footline, because the footline is typed in the bottom margin area. By the same token, the .HE command gives you a header that's in the top margin near the actual top of the sheet of paper you're using.

Something else happens when you type **[Ctl]** OP to turn off the page break display. The status line at the top of the screen changes. Instead of showing the page number and line number, it displays FC=26069 and FL=891, or something similar (see Fig. 9-9). This display is the same kind you get when you open the file with the ''N'' (edit non-document file) command instead of ''D'' from the No-File Menu. ''N'' means non-document file, and as such, is usually used when entering lists of data such as mailing lists.

The FC gives you a count of how many bytes or characters there are between the beginning of the file and the cursor location. As such, it's a quick and easy way of seeing just how much memory

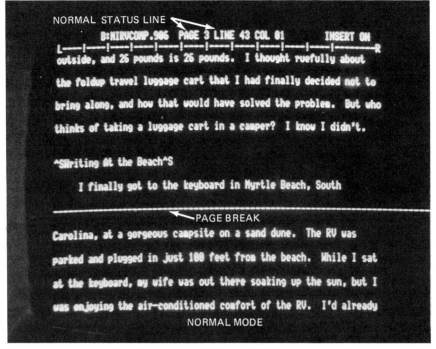

NORMAL STATUS LINE

B:NIRVCOMP.906   PAGE 3 LINE 43 COL 01   INSERT ON
L----!----!----!----!----!----!----!----!----!----!--------R
outside, and 26 pounds is 26 pounds. I thought ruefully about

the foldup travel luggage cart that I had finally decided not to

bring along, and how that would have solved the problem. But who

thinks of taking a luggage cart in a camper? I know I didn't.

^SWriting At the Beach^S

    I finally got to the keyboard in Myrtle Beach, South

--PAGE BREAK

Carolina, at a gorgeous campsite on a sand dune. The RV was

parked and plugged in just 100 feet from the beach. While I sat

at the keyboard, my wife was out there soaking up the sun, but I

was enjoying the air-conditioned comfort of the RV. I'd already

NORMAL MODE

(A)

Fig. 9-9 (A).   In normal document mode, the dashed-line page break appears at the end of
each 55 lines of text and spaces.

your file is occupying. FL indicates the number of the file line you're
on—including lines occupied by dot commands. This information is
handy for keeping track of the number of names/address files you've
entered, if you enter them as a single line per file.

Main Menu Display

The display of the Main Menu, with all of its helpful cursor movement command keys and delete functions, is automatic with most
WordStar installations. Some computer manufacturers may modify
the WordStar they supply so the default does not include this display. This is especially true of the Otrona, which has a special set of
definitions for its top row of keys (the number key row).

CHANGED STATUS LINE

B:MIRUCOMP.906 FC=4589 FL=156 COL 81   INSERT ON
L----!----!----!----!----!----!----!----!----!----!----!---------R
outside, and 26 pounds is 26 pounds. I thought ruefully about

the foldup travel luggage cart that I had finally decided not to

bring along, and how that would have solved the problem. But who

thinks of taking a luggage cart in a camper? I know I didn't.

^SWriting At the Beach^S

        I finally got to the keyboard in Myrtle Beach, South
                        NO PAGE BREAK
Carolina, at a gorgeous campsite on a sand dune. The RV was

parked and plugged in just 100 feet from the beach. While I sat

at the keyboard, my wife was out there soaking up the sun, but I

was enjoying the air-conditioned comfort of the RV. I'd already
                        ^OP MODE

(B)

Fig. 9-9 (B). By typing ^OP, you can eliminate the page break markings and change the status line to "non-document" file mode. In this mode, instead of counting lines and pages, the status line shows actual file line entry numbers and total character count.

If you feel fairly proficient with the control commands, you can get rid of the Main Menu display with the command: [Ctl] JH2. This calls up "Help" Option 2, which eliminates the Main Menu display, but will display the other menus (O, P, K, Q and J) when you type any of those keys along with the [Ctl] key. If you don't want to see those either, then type [Ctl] JH1.

10
Using WordStar's Print Command

The moment of truth—printing out your text from a WordStar file—is when you see the finished product and agonize over the mistakes you've made. Whether you're using a $2,000+ heavy-duty daisy-wheel printer such as the Diablo or Qume, a $1,300 Daisywriter, an $800 Smith-Corona or a $600 Dynax or Silver Reed—you'll be amazed by watching the printing function the first few times.

You'll also be perplexed, because there are certain things you have to learn from trial and error. These include page positioning before starting, and the limitations of your particular printer (see Fig. 10–1).

SETTING UP YOUR SOFTWARE

No matter how your WordStar is set up, you have to do some work with your CP/M utility package to set up the printer output. Your computer may have only a serial port, or a parallel port (see Fig. 10–2) and your printer may take just one or the other. If the two are compatible—and no self-respecting dealer would sell you a computer and printer that don't work together—you'll still have to look at such things as the printer setup in CP/M.

If you're using serial feed to the printer, you have to set the BAUD rate. This is the number of bits per second that the computer sends to the printer. The printer must be set to receive, understand and use the data stream at the Baud rate the computer is using. If the printer is set for 1200 Baud, for example, you have to go into your CP/M utility and set the rate.

The generic version of CP/M contains a command file called

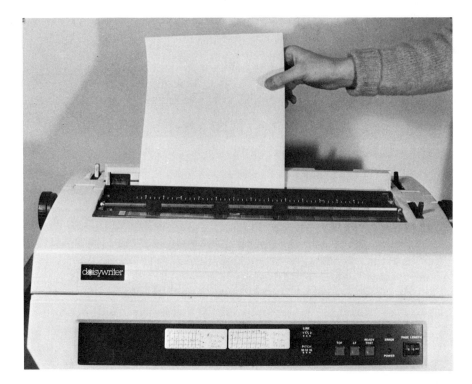

Fig. 10-1.   The actual starting position of the paper in the printer is crucial; the computer/printer combination can only work with what you give it.

BAUD.COM. In the operating system (A>), simply type BAUD **[Return]**, and this utility program will load and execute. It will present you with a string of different Baud rates and ask you to select one. You type in your answer and hit the **[Return]** key. The utility will then ask you if you want to save (or record) this parameter and will give you a (Y/N) selection. Type "Y". In some CP/M versions, you will also have to type **[Return]**, and the CP/M utility will place this new Baud rate on the Operating System portion of the disk.

Remember, changing this on one disk does not change it on the others (see Fig. 10-3). You'll have to do this on the master that you use for copying, formatting, and preparing all of your system and blank file diskettes.

Different computer manufacturers have created their own subpro-

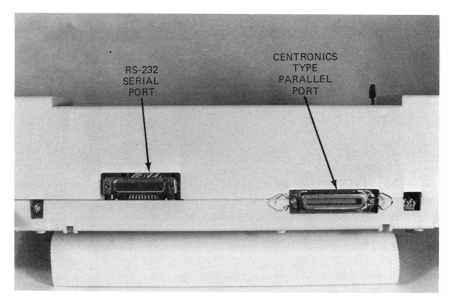

Fig. 10-2.   Some printers, such as this Star Micronics Delta 10, are equipped with both standard RS-232 serial and Centronics-type parallel ports.

grams that are more user-friendly. Kaypro, for example, uses a command file called CONFIG.COM which, when called up, presents choices and explanations. It defines different Baud rates as: most commonly used for printers, not commonly used, highest-rate used for printers, etc. All you have to do is move the cursor to the proper Baud rate, hit **[Return]** and that's that.

The Eagle II (on which this book has been written) has a CP/M utility called ASSIGN.COM, which gives you the option of not only choosing Baud rate, but choosing between one of two serial ports, or selecting one of two parallel printer ports. It also lists a number of generic printer types—invaluable in matching up the computer to the printer.

Bear in mind that if you decide to change printers, you *must* go back into whatever CP/M utility program your computer uses and change the printer parameters to match the new machine. In some cases, no change at all will be necessary.

Fig. 10-3. If your computer has both serial and parallel outputs, and you work with two different printers, it's a good idea to have separate system disks formatted for the two different kinds of printers. Changing the disk in the computer makes the printer selection.

YOUR FIRST PRINTOUT

The simplest way to print a file is to save and close your file (**[Ctl] KD**), which will take a few seconds of clicking and groaning in the disk drives while the screen status line displays the message: "WAIT". Then the No-File Menu will appear.

Make sure your printer is turned on and is loaded with paper. Then type the letter "P" (which means "Print" on the menu). The computer will then start asking questions.

First, it will ask:

NAME OF FILE TO PRINT?

Answer this with the *complete* filename, such as "XYZCO-LET.017". If you have trouble remembering filenames, bear in mind that WordStar displays them in a columnar index right below the No-File Menu. And remember also that you can't print out a file with the ".BAK" extension. If you want to print such a file, you'll have to copy it first, using WordStar's "O" (cOpy) command, and give it a filename that has some extension other than BAK.

Alternatively, you can rename this file with the "E" command (rEname) from the menu, but this can be dangerous, since then you will have no backup file on the disk. That's a decision you have to make, and if you feel that you won't do any irrevocable harm to the file, then go ahead. BAK files are sometimes just a nuisance, anyway.

After you've keystroked the filename, hit **[Return],** and the questions start. Most of them can be answered "No" by simply hitting the **[Return]** key again. And in fact, the first statement to appear on the screen is:

For default press RETURN for each question:

Now let's take a look at each question that will come up. The first question is:

DISK FILE OUTPUT (Y/N):

About 99.9 percent of the time, you'll want to default on this one by simply typing **[Return].** This statement really pulls in a PIP-like function for copying the file into a new file. If you answer "yes," then you'll have to tell WordStar the output file name, and it will create this new file *instead* of printing out. This can come in handy when using such MailMerge functions as ".AV" (Ask Variable) which is far beyond the scope of this book.

Another thing this will do is to create a "printed" version of the file on the screen—eliminating dot commands and printing special things like headers on each page, and so forth. If you want to review a file in this way, it can come in handy. But the formatted file still isn't exactly the way you'd like to see it on the printer.

While "printing" the file to disk, WordStar responds to dot commands, but the **[Ctl]** keys still appear as ^S, etc. And after all that, the file still doesn't look the way it will on the paper printout. Besides, after only a very short time using WordStar, you feel sure enough of yourself not to need a crutch of this type, if indeed you needed it at all in the first place.

The next print question is:

START AT PAGE NUMBER (RETURN for beginning)?

This is pretty self-explanatory. If you happen to be printing a 20-page file and you corrected a mistake on page 15 that doesn't carry over onto following pages and you just want to print that one page, simply type "15" **[Return]** here. Then the next question:

STOP AFTER PAGE NUMBER (RETURN for end)?

If you want to print just page 15, then answer this question too with "15" **[Return]**.

The next question may need some explanation.

USE FORM FEEDS (Y/N):

Most printers have their own "form feeds" which can find the top of the next page automatically, once the computer tells it that it has reached the bottom of the page (see Fig. 10-4). Most printers, however, will ignore their own top-of-form logic if WordStar sends out its own form feed signal. It's really up to you and the kind of printer you're using, but chances are, just hitting **[Return]** for default will work just fine. Some versions of WordStar, by the way, may not include this particular question.

Next on the board is:

SUPPRESS PAGE FORMATTING(Y/N):

You'd answer "Yes" to this only if you wanted to get a printout showing all the dot commands. The printout would also continue

Fig. 10-4.   Setting the page length on a printer like the Daisywriter is straightforward with thumbwheels. The "66" in the window is 66 lines or 11 inches.

right across any perforations in fanfold paper—not allowing any top and bottom margin for page breaks. The **[Ctl]** key commands, however, do not turn off—so instead of getting ^Sunder^S, you'd get under—nicely underscored. Same thing goes for other control character commands. Again, most of the time, you'd simply want to hit **[Return]** on this query.

Next WordStar asks a very crucial question:

PAUSE FOR PAPER CHANGE BETWEEN PAGES (Y/N):

If you're using hand-fed single sheets of paper, answer this "Y" **[Return]**. Otherwise, just hit **[Return]** again, and your continuous fanfold paper will run through just fine.

The last prompt is:

Ready printer, press RETURN:

This one is the biggie. Hitting **[Return]** is telling the computer "go." The disk will groan a little as WordStar searches for your file and starts to send it to the printer.

If you expect to default on *all* the questions, you can avoid all those questions and expected replies. After you've entered the file-name, instead of typing **[Return]**, hit "Escape." This is equivalent to defaulting on all the questions, and will immediately start the file-search and print operation.

If you only have to answer one of the questions—such as starting on page 15, you can hit "Escape" at that point instead of **[Return]**, and avoid the rest of the screen prompts.

If, by the way, you do start with page 15, WordStar will take an appreciable length of time reading through your file before it finds that page and can start to send it to the printer. The farther the page you're printing is from the *beginning* of the file, the longer this search will take.

PRINTING FROM THE FILE

Suppose you're in the middle of the file and you want to print out what you've completed without exiting from that file. First save without closing with **[Ctl] KS**. This will save everything up to your last keystroke. Then hit **[Ctl] KP**. The message, NAME OF FILE TO PRINT? will appear at the top of the screen. If you're printing the file you have open, type in that file's complete name and extension and hit **[Return]**. WordStar will then give you a warning message, telling you that you are printing from the file you are now editing, and that WordStar will print the last saved version.

Be careful here. If you're answering the individual prompts with **[Return]** keystrokes, be sure not to use multiple strokes to get down to the end of the questions quickly. It's easy to lose count, and suddenly you'll have three or four extra hard carriage returns inserted in the file. Later on, you'll wonder where they came from, and why the page breaks aren't where you wanted them to be.

You can also print from other files while you have a file open.

The procedure is identical, but you won't get a warning message. If you can't remember the exact name of the file you want to print out, after you type **[Ctl]** KP, and the prompt, NAME OF FILE TO PRINT? appears, type **[Ctl]** F, and the disk directory will be displayed.

Print Pause

If you answered "Y" to the prompt, PAUSE FOR PAPER CHANGE BETWEEN PAGES, the printer will stop after printing the first page. Assuming you're printing from the No-File Menu, this is when you load a new sheet of paper, stationery, an envelope, or whatever it is you're printing on, into the printer. You *must* position it properly; the printer can't do it for you.

Some printers will require you to feed to the bottom of the page before you start the next page. For such printers, you have to hit the "ON/OFF-LINE" button or similarly labeled control, then hit the L.F. (line feed) or the F.F. (form feed)—whichever button your printer requires that you press to get to the bottom of the page. Once this is done, *be sure to turn the printer back on line* with the ON/OFF-LINE button. Then, and only then, type the letter "P" on the computer to start printing the next page.

Note that the screen prompt changes during the print mode (see Fig. 10–5). The letter "P" on the menu changes meaning, and while the printer is running, it now means "Stop Print." If you hit "P", the printer will finish printing out whatever is in its buffer memory and then will stop. This could be just the line that it's working on, it could be two or three lines, or it could be two or three pages— depending on the size of the buffer.

When you hit "P" to stop print, and the printer finally halts, the screen will display this prompt:

TYPE "Y" TO ABANDON PRINT, "N" TO RESUME, ^U TO HOLD:

This prompt is pretty much self-explanatory. If the print operation was really screwed up and you'll have to start all over again, type "Y". This gives you a chance to correct the problem in the printer, the paper, ribbon, or whatever else went wrong.

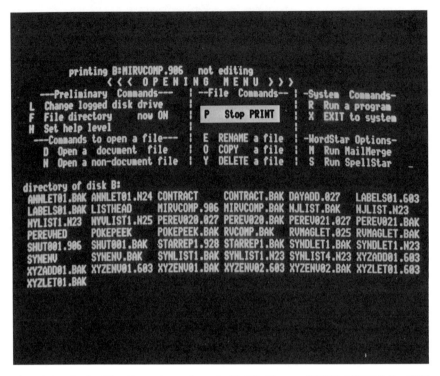

Fig. 10–5. During WordStar printout from the No-File Menu, a "STOP PRINT" (for "P") menu listing will appear. This lets you abort or pause printing operations if something is going wrong at the printer. However, if your printer has a large buffer storage capacity, typing "P" won't stop the printer for several lines.

"N" may or may not work in resuming after correcting something like a ribbon-out or paper-out situation. If the ribbon ends or gets jammed, the printer will stop automatically, and will probably beep or squawk at you. Some printers will send a signal back to the computer, and the screen will say "Print Paused" or "Print Interrupted." When you change the ribbon and type "N" to resume, the printer will probably take off right from where it stopped.

Very often, though, because you may have had to fool around with the position of the print head to change the ribbon, you'll get at least one character either missing or overstruck somewhere else on the line. You may have to abort the print operation, and restart the whole thing from the beginning of the page that got fouled up.

USING MAILMERGE

If you have the MailMerge overlay for your WordStar program, you can do a ton of special things with your computer's print operations. We won't go into the many techniques that can be used, but bear in mind that to start a MailMerge printout operation, you have to type the letter "M" from the No-File Menu, instead of the letter "P."

One of the useful features of the merge-print operation is an additional print function prompt:

Number of copies (RETURN for 1)?

```
..File D-2: XYZLET01.603
.OP
.DF XYZADD01.603
.RV NAME, COMPANY, ADDRESS, ADDRESS2, ZIP, SALUT, CLIENT


                               May 16, 1984


&NAME&
&COMPANY&
&ADDRESS&
&ADDRESS2& &ZIP&

Dear &SALUT&:

In response to your inquiry regarding our client, &CLIENT&, and
their current activities, we are pleased to send you the
enclosed information package.

As public relations counsel for &CLIENT&, we will send you
updated news and information on a regular basis to keep you
abreast of the company's activities.

We appreciate your interest in &CLIENT&, and if there is any
way we can be of further help to you, please don't hesitate to
give us a call.

                               Sincerely,


                               Adrienne Peele
                               Account Executive
AP:ea
Enclosures
.PA
```

Fig. 10-6.   MailMerge letter format provides variables between the ampersands (&) and lists the variable field names at the beginning. Note that a number of dot commands are used, and none of these is actually printed.

This can be very useful, even if you're not merge-printing. For example, in a straight, non-merge print operation, you may find that you need more than one copy printed out. Simply type "M" instead of "P" and answer the prompts appropriately. If you need three typed-out copies of a file, answer this prompt with the numeral "3". Then hit "Escape," and you're off to the races.

MailMerge itself is a pleasure to use. With it, you can combine a simple list of names and addresses into a computer-printed letter that becomes personalized. You can put "variables" into the body of the letter as well. Fig. 10–6 is a sample form for a MailMerge letter.

MailMerge is treated in greater detail in chapter 11. But if you simply regard it as an everyday working part of WordStar, you'll find a huge number of applications for it. Some of these include printing personalized form letters, mailing labels and lists, travel telephone lists, contracts and agreements typed to order, proposals— once again from forms with appropriate variables typed in.

11

Using MailMerge

MailMerge is an extra-powerful module for WordStar and adds so much versatility and capability to the basic word processing system. If you don't have MailMerge, skip this chapter.

MailMerge uses two basic "markers"—the dot command and the ampersand (&). The dot commands tell MailMerge what to do, and the "&" tells MailMerge *where* to do it.

FORM LETTERS

Any time a period appears in column 1, WordStar assumes that it is a dot command, and will not print the period or *anything else on that line.*

Look at Fig. 11-1. This is a sample form letter set up with typical MailMerge commands. The first line has two dots, which is not a command at all, but a *comment.* In this case, it is a label for your own reference so you know to what the filename and other data refer.

The second line: .OP (Omit Page number), tells WordStar not to print a page number at the bottom of the page.

The third line: .DF names the Data File where WordStar will find the variables to fill the blanks in the letter. Whatever file name you give to the Data File *must* be exactly duplicated on this line. This technique is called "nesting" and can be an invaluable tool for building mailing lists as well as keeping records.

The fourth line: .RV tells MailMerge to "Read Variables" in the six *fields* named on this line. Each word or expression between commas on this line is a *field* and must be exactly duplicated between a

```
..File D-2: XYZLET01.603
.OP
.DF XYZADD01.603
.RV NAME, COMPANY, ADDRESS, ADDRESS2, ZIP, SALUT, CLIENT


                                    May 16, 1984

&NAME&
&COMPANY&
&ADDRESS&
&ADDRESS2& &ZIP&

Dear &SALUT&:

In response to your inquiry regarding our client, &CLIENT&, and
their current activities, we are pleased to send you the
enclosed information package.

As public relations counsel for &CLIENT&, we will send you
updated news and information on a regular basis to keep you
abreast of the company's activities.

We appreciate your interest in &CLIENT&, and if there is any
way we can be of further help to you, please don't hesitate to
give us a call.

                                    Sincerely,


                                    Adrienne Peele
                                    Account Executive
AP:ea
Enclosures
.PA
```

Fig. 11-1.   Example of MailMerge form letter using "&" symbols to mark variables.

pair of ampersands (&) in the location where this information is to be printed in the letter.

The name and address sections are self-explanatory. The field labeled "CLIENT" names a company that will be typed into the letter wherever the &CLIENT& appears. Even though the company name in the CLIENT slot is long and would normally push the line beyond the right margin, WordStar will automatically wordwrap the printout so it works the right way.

The .PA at the end of the letter form indicates PAge end, and will force a page break and will form-feed the sheet of paper out of the printer with most machines.

You should print out an *unformatted* copy of any form letter that you create for a mailing with all the dot commands intact. You can do this by answering "Y" to the print prompt: SUPPRESS PAGE FORMATTING (Y/N):—so you will have a printed record of the original form with all of its dot commands and its file command structure.

Keeping copies of this kind is crucial, since they become a valuable reference source for other form letters in the future. Once you have one form that works, you don't have to keep running back to the manual or to this book to find out what to type on the computer. And you can always make changes in the letter more easily if you have a printed reference copy. Put the printout in a three-ring binder along with other important papers relating to your computer.

The Data File

Setting up a data file for the names, addresses and client references is pretty easy. Use WordStar's non-document mode (hit "N" from the No-File Menu) to set up this file. Select a filename that is easily identified and be sure that this filename is nested in the proper form letter file on the .DF line.

Each comma marks the end of a field and *will not print*. If you want a comma to be printed, the expression containing the comma must be inside quotation marks (") as is the expression: "New York, NY", 10101, in the first data listing shown in Fig. 11-2. Note that there is a comma *outside* the second quote in this example. This comma marks the end of the field that is denoted by &ADDRESS2& in the form letter.

The setup for the data file is simple: set the right margin for about 180: **[Ctl]** OR, then "180" **[Return]**. When your entries go off the screen, the screen will "scroll" horizontally—that is, the screen moves to the right along the elongated "sheet of paper" that is your file. When you finally hit the **[Return]**, the cursor will move to col-

```
Mr. Mark Duclos, Financial News, 777 Broadway, "New York, NY",
10101, Mr. Duclos, "Van Ness Oil Company, Inc."                <
Ms. Rachel Silvester, ABC Newsmakers, 120 W. 65th Street, "New
York, NY", 10023, Rachel, Computer Systems Corp.               <
Mr. Emil Gestauer, Newsmakers Syndicate, 223 E. 42nd Street, New
York NY, 10017, Mr. Gestauer, Arabesque Artists' Materials     <
```

Fig. 11-2. Variables entered into data list for the form letter in Fig. 11-1.

umn 1 of the next line and the far right (column 80) of the previous line will show a " + " sign. Everything in that file line that's beyond column 79 will be off the screen.

If, for some strange reason, you're using an earlier version of WordStar (version with a number less than 3.0), when you enter data and pass the 79th column, a " + " will appear in column 80 and the line will appear to wrap to the next line on the screen. *It's still the same line.*

The status line in non-document mode is different, too. Instead of showing the page and line numbers, it will say:

FC = 5074 FL = 170

Translation: FC is the number of characters in the file up to that point, including spaces, control characters, and hard carriage returns. FL is the File Line, and you'll find this very useful. FL 170 should also mean that it is also name and address file number 170, unless you've goofed somewhere along the line, or have inserted some special lines of instructions or labeling at the beginning of the file.

End each data file line (name, company, address, etc.) with a *hard* carriage return after the *last* entry. Do not use the return until all the data are in a file line, even though the word wrap may move some of the line to the next line on the screen.

If you are creating a long list or large data file of names and addresses for a mailing list, you may want to eliminate the extra keystrokes involved. If you can live without that comma between the city and state, you can simply type the field this way: New York NY 10101, and you will have eliminated five keystrokes. It just takes some getting used to—*not* putting the comma between city and state. Some typists have this comma so ingrained that it involves a major relearning process for them.

Be sure to proofread the data file closely for extra or missing commas. Any extra or omitted commas will foul up the letter format totally. You can end up with Ms. Rachel Silvester as the CLIENT in the letter, just by omitting one comma.

When you want to merge-print, the file you print is the one that contains the form, not the data. When the MailMerge print function reads the form letter and encounters the .DF command, it knows that it must go to the file named in that line—in our example, a file called XYZADD01.603—to find the variables to plug into all those neat areas between the ampersands (&) (see Fig. 11-3).

Printing Envelopes

Now suppose, after you've run out all those nice, neat, computer-generated letters, you find you want some envelopes, too. MailMerge can create these envelopes for you as easy as pie. The format shown in Fig. 11-4 will print addresses on number 10 envelopes using the same data file that appears in Fig. 11-2.

Taken from the top, the .. line is a "comment" and labels your form with the file disk number and the filename you've given it (XYZENV01.603).

The next line, .PL 40, provides a page length of 40 lines. This means that after the printer is finished with the address, it will line

```
                                May 16, 1984


Mr. Mark Duclos
Financial News
777 Broadway
New York, NY 10101

Dear Mr. Duclos:

In response to your inquiry regarding our client, Van Ness Oil
Company, Inc., and their current activities, we are pleased to
send you the enclosed information package.

As public relations counsel for Van Ness Oil Company, Inc., we
will send you updated news and information on a regular basis to
keep you abreast of the company's activities.

We appreciate your interest in Van Ness Oil Company, Inc., and
if there is any way we can be of further help to you, please
don't hesitate to give us a call.

                                Sincerely,


                                Adrienne Peele
                                Account Executive
AP:ea
Enclosures
```

Fig. 11-3. A sample of a mail-merged letter using the data format of Fig. 11-1 and the first data file in Fig. 11-2.

```
..File D-2: XYZENV01.603
.PL 40
.MT 16
.MB 0
.OP
.DF XYZADD01.603
.RV NAME, COMPANY, ADDRESS, ADDRESS2, ZIP, SALUT, CLIENT

                                    &NAME&
                                    &COMPANY&
                                    &ADDRESS&
                                    &ADDRESS2& &ZIP&

.PA
```

Fig. 11-4.   Sample of envelope layout using data file shown in Fig. 11-2.

feed about 20 extra lines, rolling the platen up until the envelope has been rolled right out of the printer ready for you to pluck off and lay in a stack somewhere.

The .MT 16 tells WordStar that you want a top margin of 16 lines. This will place the first line of the address on line 17—about the right location for the address on a business envelope.

The .MB 0 means there's to be no bottom margin at all—in this case, just a convention to keep WordStar happy and contented.

The command .OP tells WordStar that you don't want a page number printed on the bottom of the envelope.

The line that starts .DF (Data File) tells MailMerge the name of the file to look in for the names and addresses.

The .RV line must list *all* of the fields as they appear in the Data File—just the same way it did in the form letter. The fact that you won't be using all of those fields on the envelope is immaterial. You *must* tell MailMerge about all of the fields it will encounter in each file.

The actual print area is tabbed to a location starting on column 41—just about the right location for the address on a number 10 envelope. You can get the same result without tabbing, leaving the &NAME& etc. flush left by preceding this with another dot command: .PO 49 (Page Offset). The usual default page offset or left margin is 8 columns. With the .PO 49 line, you have just commanded WordStar to start the type on column 41 (41 columns plus 8 columns offset).

The format shown assumes that you're using envelopes that have the return address already printed on them. If you prefer to have the printer type in your return address, use the format shown in Fig. 11–5. This shows a difference in the .MT line and the physical spacing in the format itself.

The command .MT means "top margin." WordStar normally gives you six lines of top margin space before the first printed line. Using a command like .MT 16 puts the first line of the mailing address (&NAME&) on line 17—about the right distance from the top of the envelope.

Now look at Fig. 11–5. The .MT line now has a zero—no top margin lines at all. This tells WordStar to start printing the first line of your return address on the line where you set the envelope in the printer. As with the form letter, when you want to print out envelopes, you command MailMerge to print the filename that contains the *form* for the envelope you want. MailMerge will automatically go back to the data file to look for the right variables, provided you have named this data file on the .DF line in the envelope form file.

Mailing Labels

Now that you have several hundred names and addresses in your data file, suppose you want to create a mailing list out of this re-

```
..File D-2: XYZENV01.603
.PL 40
.MT 0
.MB 0
.OP
.DF XYZADD01.603
.RV NAME, COMPANY, ADDRESS, ADDRESS2, ZIP, SALUT, CLIENT
ADRIENNE PEELE
7705 S.W. 16TH AVE.
ORLANDO, FL 30705




                        &NAME&
                        &COMPANY&
                        &ADDRESS&
                        &ADDRESS2&  &ZIP&

 .PA
```

Fig. 11–5. Example of envelope layout with a typed return address instead of a preprinted return.

source? With MailMerge, it's easy as can be. A sample mailing label for one-across format is shown in Fig. 11–6.

One-across format means one label-width on peel-off tractor-feed backing (see Fig. 11–7). This format is probably easiest to create and use, although WordStar and MailMerge will permit you to create label formats for two-, three-, and even four-across. The four-across label is the most difficult for which to create a MailMerge file, and because it requires some special keyboarding techniques, we won't go into it here.

Once again, to print labels, tell MailMerge to merge-print the file named LABELS01.603 (in this example), and the correct data file will supply all the names and addresses. Printing mailing labels is a very busy operation for the computer; it reads the format, then jumps to the data file, reads the next line of variables, plugs them into the proper slots, then prints them out. It all happens pretty fast—actually almost as fast as your printer is capable of running.

ASK VARIABLE FORMAT

One of the most intriguing formats available with MailMerge is one that uses the .AV (Ask Variable) command. This can be especially useful in typing up special one-of-a-kind documents on demand, such as a contract or letter of agreement, while a client is sitting in the next office.

With this type of setup, you call up the format file, and the computer screen starts to ask you questions. You type in the answer to each one, and after you have completed the form, the printer will chatter to life and print out the finished document for you.

```
.. File D-2: LABELS01.603
.PL 6
.MT 0
.MB 0
.DF XYZADD01.603
.RV NAME, COMPANY, ADDRESS, ADDRESS2, ZIP, SALUT, CLIENT
&NAME&
&COMPANY&
&ADDRESS&
&ADDRESS2& &ZIP&
.PA
```

Fig. 11–6. Example of MailMerge format for creating one-across mailing labels.

Fig. 11-7. For short-run labels, a simple, one-across peel-off label of this type can be used in almost any printer that has a tractor feed.

If you want to keep a disk file copy of this special contract with the appropriate answers plugged in, then answer "Y" to the first MailMerge print prompt that asks DISK FILE OUTPUT (Y/N): when you first order up this file. It will then "print" the filled-in form in its own file, which you can then print out as many times as you like.

Here's how it works:

Fig. 11-8 shows a sample letter of intent (a short-form contract) using the .AV commands. Note that whenever &COMPANY& appears in the contract form, the full name of the company will be printed out.

Let's try answering the questions. First, from the No-File Menu, stroke "M" for merge-print. The prompt will ask the name of the

```
.. File D-2: CONTRACT
.OP
.AV "Enter today's date:", DATE
.AV "Enter company officer name:", NAME
.AV "Enter officer's title:", TITLE
.AV "Enter company name:", NAME
.AV "Enter company street address:", ADDRESS
.AV "Enter company's city and state:", ADDRESS2
.AV "Enter company's ZIP code:", ZIP
.AV "Enter fee in dollars:", FEE
.AV "Enter salutation form:", SALUT
.AV "Enter startup date:", STARTUP DATE
                                     &DATE&

&NAME&
&TITLE&
&COMPANY&
&ADDRESS&
&ADDRESS2& &ZIP&

Dear &SALUT&:

This letter of intent will serve as a binding contract between
&COMPANY& and Thurgood Associates, Inc., 200 East 42nd Street,
New York, NY 10017 in which &COMPANY& agrees to retain Thurgood
Associates as its public relations counsel.

The term of this agreement is to last a minimum of six months
and may be reopened for renegotiation at any time before or
after the six months' period has expired.

For these services, &COMPANY& agrees to pay Thurgood Associates,
Inc. the sum of $&FEE& per month commencing on &STARTUP DATE&
plus any and all reasonable expenses accrued in the course of
acting as public relations counsel.  Extraordinary expenses will
be cleared with &COMPANY& before such expenditures are made.

This contract is subject to cancellation by either party
provided 30 days' notice is tendered by the party desiring the
cancellation.

_____        _____
&NAME&, &TITLE&                Roscoe Thurgood, President
&COMPANY&                      Thurgood Associates, Inc.

_____        _____
     Witness                          &DATE&
.PA
```

Fig. 11-8. MailMerge format for typing a contract using the "Ask Variable" dot command (.AV).

file, and since we have simply called this file "CONTRACT", just type CONTRACT **[Return]**.

Answer the screen prompts from MailMerge; make sure a letter-head is loaded in the printer, and start answering questions.

The first question will be:
Enter today's date:

Answer with the date: February 17, 1984
The next question will be:

Enter company officer name:

Answer each question appropriately with name, address, city and

February 17, 1984

```
Peter Langenshein
President
Lang-Micro Industries, Inc.
703 River Road
Pittsburgh, PA 12708

Dear Peter:

This letter of intent will serve as a binding contract between
Lang-Micro Industries, Inc. and Thurgood Associates, Inc., 200
East 42nd Street, New York, NY 10017 in which Lang-Micro
Industries, Inc. agrees to retain Thurgood Associates as its
public relations counsel.

The term of this agreement is to last a minimum of six months
and may be reopened for renegotiation at any time before or
after the six months' period has expired.

For these services, Lang-Micro Industries, Inc. agrees to pay
Thurgood Associates, Inc. the sum of $2,500.00 per month
commencing on March 1, 1984, plus any and all reasonable
expenses accrued in the course of acting as public relations
counsel.  Extraordinary expenses will be cleared with Lang-
Micro Industries, Inc. before such expenditures are made.

This contract is subject to cancellation by either party
provided 30 days' notice is tendered by the party desiring the
cancellation.


Peter Langenshein, President        Roscoe Thurgood, President
Lang-Micro Industries, Inc.         Thurgood Associates, Inc.



        Witness                         February 17, 1984
.PA
```

Fig. 11-9. Finished merge printout of contract from the format shown in Figure 11-8.

state, etc. The form of salutation may be simply a first name if Ros-coe Thurgood is already on a first-name basis with the client company president or whoever is signing the contract form. The final printout will look something like Fig. 11-9.

MailMerge has many other capabilities and variations—all depending on the way you use the dot commands. There are some really fascinating tricks that dot commands will let you perform on the computer, and this is one area where it pays to get creative. The examples in this chapter will give you an idea of what you can do with MailMerge.

To find out more about the command structure and some of the neat tricks, read the WordStar manual, or at least read the chapter on MailMerge. True, you may not understand all of it, but it can really fire up your imagination.

12
Quick Crib Sheets for WordStar

Okay. You've got the computer all plugged in and you have your backup and working disks made and you have a blank formatted disk for your files. You're ready and rarin' to go. But you don't want to take a lot of time with the manuals or even with reading this book. Here's a quick setup to get you going.

GETTING INTO WORDSTAR

Fire up your computer.
Put a systems/WordStar disk in Drive A.
Put a blank, formatted file disk in Drive B.
If your system is self-booting, A⟩ will appear on the screen.
If your system is not self-booting, press the RESET button.
A⟩ should appear.
Type WS **[Return]**
The computer will click and groan, the screen will go blank for a few seconds, and then the first WordStar message will appear on the screen along with a lot of information about copyright.
WAIT.
After a few more seconds, the disk drives will click and groan again, and the WordStar protocol will come up on the screen, listing your computer or a lookalike, the printer or equivalent, and the type of communications protocol.
WAIT.
After a few seconds more, the WordStar "No-File" or "Main Menu" will appear along with a directory of the files on that disk.

At this point, you are logged into Drive A—the system/programs disk.

You want to log into Drive B.

Hit "L"

A prompt will appear telling you to type the Drive letter and a colon. Type: B: [Return] (that's a *colon,* not a semi-colon—use the SHIFT key).

A new directory will come up under the menu labeled Disk B. You're ready to create your first file.

USING THE CONTROL KEY

The "Control" key is used frequently in setups and calling up special commands in combination with other keys on the keyboard. Each time you see [Ctl] followed by a letter, it means you should hold the Control key down and then press that letter key. In the WordStar command summaries, they represent the Control key with a caret (^) before the letter. Thus ^PS means hold the Control key while typing the PS keys. In our lists here, we simply say, [Ctl] PS. The reason we do this: there is already a caret key on most computers—the uppercase of the numeral 6. We do it without the caret to avoid confusion for beginners.

OPENING A FILE

Type the "D" key (open Document file). This will get you into an existing file or let you create a new file.

WordStar will ask you: NAME OF FILE TO EDIT?

Answer with the *exact* filename of an old file or the new file such as:

XYZLET01.603 [Return].

The computer will click and groan a bit, and the file will suddenly appear on the screen. If it's a new file, the screen will say NEW FILE for a couple of seconds and then your file will appear as a blank page. On top will be the status line; below that will be the ruler/TAB Line; below that will be your command menu.

NOTE: Some versions of WordStar that have been "customized"

by the computer manufacturer may not display this command or the "Main Menu." If all you see is the status line and the ruler line, type **[Ctl]** JH3, and you'll get the Main Menu display.

FILE SETUP

To set the typing parameters you need, do the following:
[Ctl] OJ turns off right-margin justification to give you ragged right.
[Ctl] OH turns off hyphen-help for greater speed in reformatting.
[Ctl] OR lets you reset the right margin. You might want to leave it alone your first couple of times around.
[Ctl] OS lets you change from single-spacing to double-, triple- or whatever spacing you want, up to nine spaces.
If you want to change TAB stops, which are set every five spaces on the ruler line at startup, first CLEAR the old TAB stops.
Hit **[Ctl]** ON
WordStar will ask you which stops to clear.
Type "A" **[Return]**
This will clear *all* TAB stops.
Now suppose you want to set TABS at columns 6 and 41—good for paragraph indents and for tabbing to type a date, letter close, etc.
Hit **[Ctl]** OI, then the number 6 **[Return]**
Hit **[Ctl]** OI again, then the number 41 **[Return]**
If you're setting up a table and want to set TAB stops at column headings, move the cursor to the first column heading, hit **[Ctl]** OI and then [Escape]. This will set the TAB at the cursor location.

SAVE FREQUENTLY

If the phone rings, or you have to go to the john or something, *save the file.* All it takes is **[Ctl]** KS. This saves the file without taking you out of it.
Then to get back to the exact spot where you left off, type **[Ctl]** QP. It's that simple.
To save the file and close it and return to the No-File or Main Menu, type **[Ctl]** KD.
Remember, **[Ctl]** KD gets you out no matter what, and won't destroy anything.

SETTING UP PAGE FOOTINGS AND HEADERS

If you're doing a multiple-page document, such as a report or a manuscript, chances are you don't want a page number on page 1, but would like to number all the following pages in a particular location. WordStar ordinarily will place a neat page number in the middle of the bottom margin of each page. You turn this off by placing the .OP at the beginning of the file.

Now suppose you want to type a running head like:

Duclos Chemical Company Annual Report - Page 2

After the report is complete, or after you're pretty much satisfied with the first couple of pages, place the cursor on column 1 line 1 of page 2. If there's some text there, hit **[Ctl]** N once or twice. This inserts a hard carriage return without moving the cursor.

Now type .HE (HEader) with the period in column 1. Find the proper location for the rest of the text in the header, and type:

.HE Duclos Chemical Company Annual Report - Page #

WordStar will plug in the proper page number for the # symbol, and the same header and running page number will be neatly printed at the top of every page that follows.

To turn the header off, type .HE anywhere you like, as long as the period is in column 1. This stops the header printout.

Setting Up Footlines

Running footlines in the bottom margin work the same way as headers. The key here is .FO at the bottom of the first page to carry the footline. You don't *have* to plug in a running page number on headers or footlines.

Suppose you just want to have "(Continued next page)" centered on the bottom of the page.

Get down to the last line of this page (Use **[Ctl]** N to move a line or two of text out of the way) and type: (Continued next page)

Next type **[Ctl]** OC, and this will automatically center the material you just typed.

Now type **[Ctl]** QS, and this will move the cursor back to column 1 of the same line.

Now type .FO and you'll see the page-break ruler line immediately jump down one line. This always happens when you insert any kind of dot command on the last line of a page.

With this done, WordStar will now print the continued message on the bottom of each page.

CAREFUL—you don't want this to print on the last page of your report. So turn off the footline control on the last page with a .FO and nothing printed after it.

Once again, be sure the period is in column 1.

In general, the last page of a multipage report that uses both headers and footlines should have these dot commands after the end of the text:

.HE
.FO
.PA

The .PA forces the end of the page, and will feed the paper up through the printer to the end of the sheet.

REFORMATTING A FILE

Suppose you have a file that you've done in draft form, double-spaced for ease of editing, and with ragged right margins. Now you want to single-space it and have the right margins justified (ruler-straight).

First change to single-spacing.

Type **[Ctl]** OS 1

The flag on the right-hand end of the status line that said LINE SPACING 2 will disappear.

Next type **[Ctl]** OJ. This turns the justification toggle back on, if it was turned off to begin with.

Do you want to hyphenate long words? If so, type **[Ctl]** OH to turn the hyphen-help back on. If not, leave it off.

Now bring your cursor to the beginning of the file.

Type **[Ctl]** B, and keep doing it. You will work down through the file, with the cursor stopping only at hard carriage returns or on a long word needing to be hyphenated (if hyphen-help is ON).

You have absolute control at this point, since the **[Ctl]** B reformatting command will only reformat a maximum of one paragraph at a time. You can stop to make changes and corrections as you go along.

BE CAREFUL of the **[Ctl]** B reformatting control. If you have tabular matter, columns with special dimensions that you worked hard to arrange, and any special text—skip past them with **[Ctl]** Z. DO NOT USE **[Ctl]** B on these delicately constructed sections; **[Ctl]** B will wreck them.

FILE OPERATIONS

The K menu works with block operations. Here are the file commands:

[Ctl] KS—saves the file without exiting. You can return to your original cursor location with **[Ctl]** QP.

[Ctl] KD—saves the file and exits to the No-File (Main) Menu.

[Ctl] KX—saves the file and exits from WordStar to the Operating System, giving you the A⟩ or B⟩.

[Ctl] KQ—abandons the file and doesn't save any changes.

[Ctl] KJ—deletes a file other than the one you're working on.

[Ctl] KO—lets you copy a file external to the one you're working on.

[Ctl] KR—lets you read another file.

[Ctl] KW—lets you copy a marked block to another, external file.

[Ctl] KP—lets you print any file without exiting from the file you're working on. You may also print the file you're working on in its last saved version.

[Ctl] KE—lets you rename another file.

BLOCK OPERATIONS

You can move, delete, copy, create separate files from, and read files into the open file with the block commands. To work with text within the file, mark the block to be used:

[Ctl] KB places a marker ⟨B⟩ at the beginning of the block—wherever your cursor is when you hit [Ctl] KB.

[Ctl] KK marks the end of the block ⟨K⟩. Both markers must be in place for any block commands to have an effect.
Memory aid: ⟨B⟩loc⟨K⟩—B is the first letter of the word BlocK. K is the last letter.

Move the cursor to the new location where you want the marked block to move.

Type [Ctl] KV. That's all there is to it.

[Ctl] KC will Copy the block to the cursor location without moving the original marked block.

[Ctl] KY will delete (erase) the entire marked block.

[Ctl] KW will Write (copy) the marked block into a separate file. You have to answer WordStar's prompt with a new filename for this block. If the file already exists, you are asked if you want to overwrite. If you answer "Y", anything that was already in that file will be erased.

[Ctl] KR will Read any other file you name in response to WordStar's prompt, NAME OF FILE TO READ? The entire file will appear in the file you're currently working on, beginning at the cursor location. You may just need portions of this added material and can use the block markers to delete the rest.

[Ctl] KH will Hide the block markers that may be in place. It also effectively turns them off, so the other [Ctl] K block operations will not work.

[Ctl] KN turns on the columnar limits for marking a block. Use this if you want to move a *column* but not the entire width of the page. Type [Ctl] KN *before* you place the markers ⟨B⟩ and ⟨K⟩.

NOTE: With certain terminals and computers, marking a block will turn on the highlight for that section—the image will reverse itself. If your screen normally displays green letters on a black background, the highlighted material will appear as black letters on a green background. Some people like this feature; others don't. If your computer highlights and you don't like it at first, stick with it. You'll find that you really appreciate this feature after a while.

The K menu also lets you place up to 10 numbered markers in the text (numbers 0 through 9). To place a number 1, type [Ctl] K1, and a ⟨1⟩ will appear at the cursor location. You can return to this number any time by stroking [Ctl] Q1. With some computers, you may have to take your finger off the [Ctl] key *after* stroking the Q and *before* stroking the numeral.

You can also quickly move to the beginning or end of a marked block with [Ctl] QB (beginning) or [Ctl] QK (end). As with the numerals, you may have to remove your finger from the [Ctl] key before stroking the B or the K.

FIND AND REPLACE

Sometimes, just finding something in the text is all you want to do.

[Ctl] QF is the Find control. You will be asked what you want to find. Type out the word or expression *exactly* as it appears, since WordStar can't make a near match—only an exact match. Keep it short; the temporary memory used for a "Find" command will hold a maximum of 30 characters.

[Ctl] QA is the Find and Replace command. Again, you have to be very precise about what it is you want to find. You must also be very precise about what you want to replace it with. If you try replacing the word "the" for example, it will also be replaced where it occurs in the middle of other words such as "other." To replace such a word accurately and only when it's a separate word, when you're asked what to find, type a *space* before and after the word. This way WordStar will only find "the" when it's preceded by a space. Be sure to include the same spaces for the replacement word.

OPTIONS are what make this function so versatile. If you type no options, but just the [Return] key, then the search will stop at the first instance and ask you if you want to replace it or not (Replace Y/N)? Then it will go on to the next occurrence of the word. Options consist of letters that have special meaning.

"G" means "Global"—the [Ctl] QA operation will find and replace *every* occurrence of the selected word in the entire file.

"N" means "don't ask," but go ahead and replace it. Thus the operation becomes automatic.

"B" means search Backwards, which you must do if you're starting from the end of the file.

"U" means ignore "Upper or lower case." Thus this would find "The" as well as "the" or "THE".

"W" means "Whole words only," so [Ctl] QA wouldn't replace "the" in "other" but only when it stands by itself.
One further option is *number*. By typing any numeral in the options you can look for that number occurrence of a word. Thus if you typed "8", WordStar would stop at every eighth occurrence of "the", ignoring all the others.

[Ctl] L will restart the operation, telling WordStar to start again after it's found the word you were searching for. It will go on to the next one and stop there.

[Ctl] U and [Escape] will stop the whole operation.

NOTE: If you're using a GN option for replacing a lot of occurrences in the file, and you don't want to watch it all happening, you can hit any key (we suggest the SPACE bar). The screen will freeze where it is, and WordStar will do the replace operation at lightning speed without showing you what it's doing.

QUICK-KEY OPERATIONS

The Q or "Quick" menu lets you perform a number of special operations. The [Ctl] Q keys *always* work in combination with some other key, so we'll be showing double letters here.

[Ctl] QS—moves cursor to far left end of line.
[Ctl] QD—moves cursor to far right end of line.
[Ctl] QR—moves cursor to beginning of the file.
[Ctl] QC—moves cursor to end of the file.
[Ctl] QY—deletes entire line to the right of the cursor.
[Ctl] Q-DEL—deletes entire line to the left of the cursor.
[Ctl] QF—find.

[Ctl] QA—find and replace.
[Ctl] QE—moves cursor to top of screen.
[Ctl] QX—moves cursor to bottom of screen.
[Ctl] QQ—repeats command; speed can be varied by tapping numeral.
[Ctl] QL—find misspelled word (only if you have SpellStar program).
[Ctl] Q1—find place marker ⟨1⟩.

PRINT COMMANDS

The "P" or Print menu has many two-key controls that appear on the screen as a control caret and just one letter: ^S, ^B, etc. Many of these are useful during actual writing. With some of them, you have to turn the function off—such as ^S (underscore) and ^B (boldface). Here's a summary:

[Ctl] PS—(on/off) underscores all *typed* material, but not spaces.
[Ctl] PB—(on/off) boldfaces.
[Ctl] PD—(on/off) doublestrikes characters.
[Ctl] PV—(on/off) subscript characters.
[Ctl] PT—(on/off) superscript characters.
[Ctl] PX—(on/off) strikeout characters (with slashes).
[Ctl] PH—overprints single character (useful for foreign accents).
[Ctl] PM—overprints entire line (useful for underscoring).
[Ctl] PC—makes printer pause and wait for "resume" command.

Let's look at a couple of these. **[Ctl]** PS places a ^S on the line. If you want to underscore several words, it will look like this in the text: ^Sthese words will be underscored, but not the spaces between.^S

If you want to underscore words and spaces, you can type an underscore between the words instead of hitting the space bar. An easier way is to use the **[Ctl]** PM. When you reach the end of a line that contains material to be underscored, instead of hitting the **[Return]**, hit **[Ctl]** PM. A minus sign (−) will appear at the right of the screen and the cursor will be on the line below, just as though you had hit the **[Return]**. Space the cursor over until it's under the material you want underscored, and then, holding down the shift key, hold down the underscore key until you have enough for all the material to be underscored. Then hit the **[Return]**. It will look something like this: This sentence contains some material that is to be underscored. —

——————————————————————— <

Suppose you want to overstrike a letter, for example, to make a cent symbol, which most daisy wheels don't contain. You can create this by overstriking the lowercase letter "c" with a slash "/". Type: c **[Ctl]** PH/

On screen, it will look like this: c^H/. On the printer, it will look like this: ¢.

Superscripts and subscripts depend a great deal on the kind of printer you're using. Some printers will respond to a superscript command by rolling the paper down a half-line for degree symbols, trademarks, etc. Others that don't have this capability will simply type the superscripted material in the line above, while some will print it on the same line as though you had done absolutely nothing.

A superscripted TM (trademark) will look like this on the screen: Kodak^TTM^T

The ^T is what you get when you type **[Ctl]** PT. It is a *toggle*— that is, it turns the function on, and then must be told to turn it off, just like a toggle switch.

There are many other "tricks" you can get your printer to perform with WordStar in the saddle, but they are beyond the scope of this book. The ones in this chapter, at least, will help you to get started.

13
Using Sorting Programs

Sorting programs are usually part of what is called a "data base" management program—such as DataStar and ReportStar from MicroPro. Programs such as these are pretty much self-teaching, and we won't deal with them here. When you tell such a program to do a particular kind of sorting operation, it does it with few, if any questions asked.

Not so with SuperSort—also from MicroPro. This is an extraordinarily powerful sorting program that's relatively inexpensive, and if you happen to have it in your software library, you've got a gem—provided you know how to use it. And that's the tough part, since this program, for all of its power and versatility, comes with an instruction manual that is best understood by people who have a degree in computer science.

SETTING UP THE DATA BASE

If you've set up any data base files to use with your MailMerge operations, you've already got the beginnings of an excellent mailing list and the source of a lot of other information. You can transfer MailMerge files onto another disk and expand the individual listings with special information and sorting keys for future selection.

A sorting key is something you decide on for picking out certain people or companies or customers or what-have-you for mailings at some future date. The sorting key can consist of a word, a couple of code letters and/or numbers—anything you choose.

We're going to make an assumption here. We'll assume that you have established a particular format for your data base, using commas to separate the fields, since you probably set it up that way for the original customized letter mailings with MailMerge.

We'll set up a sample 10-field data base here, laid out as shown in Fig. 13-1.

Each field is marked by a comma. The person's name has been split into two fields, so it's possible to do an alphabetic sort on the person's last name (Field #2). The company name is in Field #3, the ZIP code is Field #6, and the phone number is Field #7.

Fields 8, 9 and 10 indicate sorting and selection codes that may or may not be used in the future to pick out certain people from this list. The combination of letters and their meaning can be whatever you decide. If you have no code or no phone number, you can leave the field blank, but *you must put a comma there even if the field is blank.*

SETTING UP THE MAILING LABEL

The mailing label setup is identical to the one we did in chapter 11, except for the first line, which now has two fields in it. This is because we split the person's name into two fields for sorting convenience, but we want to put the names together on the label.

A one-across label for this kind of data base would look like the format shown in Fig. 13-2.

The one difficulty with using a program like SuperSort is the fact that it fills up available disk space very quickly. Unless you're working with at least 500 K of space per diskette, you have to watch your available storage *very carefully* and must erase temporary and old files before proceeding to any new sorting routines. The alternative

```
Mr. Henry, Clay, Adams and Company, 333 So. Fourth St., Campbell CA,
FIELD 1     2      3                  4                   5

95008, 408-537-0290, flt, cust, cash
6       7             8    9     10                        HARD RETURN
```

Fig. 13-1. Typical field layout for non-document file data entry. The underscores and numbers do not appear on the screen but are for identification. 1 = first name; 2 = last name; 3 = company name; 4 = street or P.O. box address; 5 = city and state with no comma between; 6 = ZIP code; 7 = phone number; 8, 9 and 10 are special key sorting fields. When printing labels, fields 7-10 do not print, but are available for making up files, data lists, Rolodex cards, etc.

```
.PL  6
.MT  0
.MB  0
.DF  XYZADD01.603
.RV  NAME1, NAME2, COMPANY, ADDRESS, ADDRESS2, ZIP, PHONE,
     SORT1, SORT2, SORT3
&NAME1&  &NAME2&
&COMPANY&
&ADDRESS&
&ADDRESS2&  &ZIP&
.PA
```

Fig. 13-2.   One-across label format using the data base field entry layout shown in Fig. 13-1. Note that just the first six data fields are used from each data file. Since the others are not specified in the .RV line, or blocked out as variables between ampersands, they will not print.

is to move to a blank disk, and this can get very expensive after a very short time.

NAMING FILES

Filenames may seem very inconsequential, but with sorting programs, you'll end up with the same file in several different kinds of sequences, and you can pick filenames that can tell you the file sequence at a glance.

Take, for example, the file shown in Fig. 13-1. Let's key the first part of the filename: XYZADD—which can mean the address file for XYZ Company. The 01 can mean the "raw" file of unsorted information.

Now suppose you want to sort it on Field #2—that is, sort it in alphabetic order by the person's last name. You could name such a new file: "XYZADD02"—which tells you at a glance that the file is sorted on Field # 2. Add the extension: .603 for the date code, and you know that this file was last updated and sorted on June 3.

If, on the other hand, you want to do a sort in ZIP code order, you would name your file after the ZIP code field, Field #6—and the name would be: "XYZADD06.603".

Now let's try a couple of sorting routines, using MicroPro's SuperSort program. First, you must get into your Operating System (A⟩). We'll assume that you have the sorting program on Disk A and the files on Disk B. Type B: [Return] and you'll get B⟩ on the screen.

Now type A:SORT [Return]

The disk drive will whirr and groan a bit, and then the SuperSort copyright information will come up on the screen. It will look something like this:

MicroPro SUPERSORT Release 1.50 Serial SS08354RTER
COPYRIGHT (C) 1980 MICROPRO INTERNATIONAL
*

That asterisk (*) in column 1 is SuperSort's way of telling you that it's ready and wants instructions.

You will have to type five or six lines of instructions. When you finish each line of instructions, type **[Return]**, and if the instructions are in the proper format, you'll get another * on the next line. SuperSort is asking for the next line of instructions.

It makes no difference in what order you put these command lines, as long as you get all of the instructions entered in acceptable format and syntax.

One thing about SuperSort—it only requires the first three letters of a command word, the same as with any CP/M command structure. Now let's start with the INPut line.

The INPut line tells SuperSort the outer parameters of *one line* of your data file—the maximum number of characters in the line and the fact that you end the line with a hard carriage return.

If you have a maximum line length of 160 characters, for example, you can type the input line this way:

*INP = 160, CR-DEL **[Return]**

INP and INPUT are the same. You're telling SuperSort that the INP line equals a maximum of 160, and that it's carriage-return delimited (CR-DEL). That's all you need for the first line of instructions.

Next, tell SuperSort the name of the file from which you're going to get the data for sorting:

*SOR = XYZADD01.603 **[Return]**

You're telling SuperSort to SORt file XYZADD01.603. If the source file is on another disk, such as Disk A, while you're on Disk B, tell it:

*SOR = A:XYZADD01.603 **[Return]**

Next, name the file where the sorted data will end up. Let's assume it's an alphabetic sort by company name (Field #3):

*OUT = XYZADD03.603 **[Return]**

Translation: the OUTput file from the SuperSort will be named XYZADD03.603 **[Return]**

Now, tell SuperSort which field to sort and how to sort it:

*KEY = #4,20,ASCending **[Return]**

Let's look at this line a little more closely. The word "KEY" should be self-explanatory. You're telling SuperSort that the sorting key Field is #4. The comma separates it from the next statement which tells SuperSort the maximum number of characters it's likely to find in Field #4. The last statement means start with A and end up with Z (ASCending). If you wanted reverse alphabetic order, you could say "DEScending".

The very last command needs no explanation:

*GO **[Return]**

And go it will. The disks will whirr and click and groan and work their fingers to the bone, sorting and rearranging much faster than the most whiz-bang secretary leafing through file cards.

In a very short time, this message (or something like it) will appear on the screen:

86 RECORDS SORTED
OUTPUT FILE SIZE 9K
*** SORT/MERGE COMPLETE ***

Okay, you did it! Now let's recap the set of instructions you used:

A⟩SORT **[Return]**

(Copyright data on screen)

*INP = 160, CR-DEL **[Return]**
*SOR = XYZADD01.603 **[Return]**
*OUT = XYZADD03.603 **[Return]**

*KEY = #3,20,ASCEND **[Return]**
*GO **[Return]**

One other thing—if you make a mistake in any of the entries, such as not telling the computer some important parameter, SuperSort will print an error message. You don't have to do the whole list over again—just the line with the mistake in it.

ZIP CODE SORT

If you want to sort your list by ZIP code to take advantage of the lower postage rates possible, you can simply change the key command line. It would look like this:

*INP = 160, CR-DEL **[Return]**
*SOR = XYZADD01.603 **[Return]**
*OUT = XYZADD06.603 **[Return]**
*KEY = # 6,10,ASCEND **[Return]**
*GO **[Return]**

Note that the OUT line changed slightly; the filename was changed to reflect the Field #6 sort for easy identification. Thus XYZADD03 became instead XYZADD06.

The KEY line was changed to #6, and the maximum number of characters changed to 10—the maximum now used with expanded ZIP codes.

If you have any foreign addresses in your data base, you should try to arrange them so the name of the country appears in Field #6. This way, they will all be sorted *after* the domestic addresses, and will be in alphabetic order by country. This is because of the way the sorting routine operates.

Each letter of the alphabet has an ASCII number, and the numbers ascend with the letter of the alphabet. When the computer does a sort, it sorts according to ASCII code order. This really works, since Z has a much higher number than A. But numerals themselves have lower ASCII numbers than the letters of the alphabet. Because of this, when there's a sort that involves both letters and numerals, the numerals will always be sorted first.

MERGING LISTS TOGETHER

If you have several different short lists, which you've most likely compiled in the process of answering requests or doing specialized tailored computer letters, at some point, you'll want to merge (combine) these lists into one long list. SuperSort lets you do this. Suppose you have three lists with these names: XYZADD01.603, ABCADD01.604, JKLADD01.605, and you want to combine them into one list to be named: COMADD06.605.

Notice that the new file has an 06 ending, meaning that it's being sorted in ZIP code sequence. Even though you may only want to combine the lists at first, SuperSort demands some kind of sorting key in the list of instructions, so while you're merging, you might as well perform a useful sorting operation. Here's what you do:

*MERge = XYZADD01.603, ABCADD01.604, JKLADD01.605 **[Return]**

You have just told SuperSort the names of the files you want to merge (MER).

*INP = 160, CR-DEL **[Return]**
*OUT = COMMADD06.605 **[Return]**
*KEY = #6,10,ASC **[Return]**
*GO **[Return]**

If everything is done according to the proper SuperSort syntax, the computer disk drives will start to whirr and chatter. After a little while, the screen may flash a message like this:

333 RECORDS MERGED
OUTPUT FILE SIZE 15K
*** SORT/MERGE COMPLETE ***

Now here's the touchy part. In spite of the fact that the SuperSort program requires that you enter a KEY code, sometimes, during a merge operation, it may not always perform the sort you ordered. Sometimes it does; sometimes it doesn't. This is one of the quirks of this program that you learn to live with.

Check the new file. If it has been ZIP-code sorted, you're ahead of the game. If it hasn't, then just put it through the sorting routine we outlined earlier. But rename the source filename first to read something like: COMADD01.605

You can change the name from the Operating System like this:

A〉REN COMADD01.605 = COMADD06.605 **[Return]**

That's all there is to it. You have just renamed the file.

Now you have to run this program again to get the true sort that you need. So do this:

A〉SORT

(Copyright statement)

*INP = 160, CR-DEL **[Return]**
*SOR = COMADD01.605 **[Return]**
*OUT = COMADD06.605 **[Return]**
*KEY = #6,10, ASC **[Return]**
*GO **[Return]**

Look familiar? It's the same old ZIP-code sorting command sequence, but with the SOR and OUT lines changed slightly to accommodate the new filenames.

Making Sort Selections

After you've created a monster by merging several shorter lists into a much longer list, there will come a time when you want to extract some of the names—but not all—for a specific mailing or canvass. SuperSort contains the means for making these selections, provided you've had the foresight to plug something into one of those "extra" sort selection fields that we suggested you use.

If you look back at Fig. 13-1, you will see that there are three special fields—8, 9 and 10—that we suggested you put into the data line for selection.

Suppose you want to pull out all the cash-with-order customers on the list. You may have entered these simply as "cash" in Field

#10 as suggested in Fig. 13-1. If that's the case, this is what the command sequence will look like:

A⟩SORT

(Copyright notice)

*INP = 160, CR-DEL **[Return]**
*SOR = COMADD01.605 **[Return]**
*OUT = COMADD06.605 **[Return]**
*KEY = #6,10,ASC **[Return]**
*SEL = FIELD #10 = "cash" **[Return]**
*GO **[Return]**

Notice the added command line right before "GO"? "SEL" is another three-letter shortening of the command, in this case, SELect. SEL must equal a particular field number, which in turn must equal the *precise* contents of the field you want to select—and this *must* be in quotes. As always, this command line can be *anywhere* in the order sequence, as long as you enter it before the "GO" command line.

As usual, the disk drives will click and hum, and after what seems like an interminable wait (actually, SuperSort is very fast), the screen will flash something like this:

333 RECORDS INPUT FOR SORT
   174 SORT RECORDS EXCLUDED OR NOT SELECTED
159 RECORDS SORTED
OUTPUT FILE 15K
*** SORT/MERGE COMPLETE ***

Note that a certain number of records were selected and others rejected. Those selected were sorted according to the command in the KEY line.

SELECTING ZIP CODE GROUPS

Suppose you want to do a mailing to a particular geographic area of the country? You can pick out these areas very easily with SuperSort. Using the filenames COMADD01.605 as the source, first you have to determine the ZIP code range. In this example, we're going to do a mailing to New York State only, which has a ZIP range of 10000 to 11999. We'll call the output file COMADDNY.605, in which the NY at the end indicates the kind of sort we're doing. Here's how to do the selection:

A⟩SORT **[Return]**

(Computer prints copyright data)

*INP = 160, CR-DEL **[Return]**
*SOR = COMADD01.605 **[Return]**
*OUT = COMADDNY.605 **[Return]**
*KEY = #6,10,ASCEND **[Return]**
*SEL = FIELD #6, BT "10000", "12000" **[Return]**
*GO **[Return]**

By this time, you've probably gotten used to hearing the computer click and groan while it's sorting. Depending on the model you're using, the SuperSort lets it handle about 10 files per second, on average. Thus the list of 369 names that we're sorting in this sample will take about 35–40 seconds to complete.

Then you'll see a message like this:

369 RECORDS INPUT FOR SORT
   237 SORT RECORDS EXCLUDED OR NOT SELECTED
132 RECORDS SORTED
OUTPUT FILE SIZE 13K
*** SORT/MERGE COMPLETE ***

You now have a sorted file of 132 names and addresses for people in New York State only, and they're arranged in ZIP-code sequence.

Let's look at the SEL command line for a moment.

*SEL = FIELD #6, BT "10000", "12000"

You have told the computer to select Field # 6 (the Zip code field) and only those numbers between ("BT") 10000 and 12000. You *must* enclose the sort number boundaries in quotes for the selection to work; otherwise, the computer will gripe at you with comments like:

ERROR S42: INVALID LINE TERMINATION

And it will even mark the error point above the error message itself with a little caret (^).

Remember, if you make an error, you do *not* have to retype all the entries—just the line where you made the mistake. Then you can continue entering the other command lines and finally the "GO". If it won't go, SuperSort will give you another error message of some kind.

There are many other special things you can do with SuperSort, but we've tried to highlight the most useful features and functions here. To get more complex routines, you'll have to live with the user's manual for a few weeks (or months). Good luck!

14
Housekeeping Routines for CP/M and WordStar

While using a computer can eliminate a ton of unnecessary paper-work, somehow, in the process of eliminating paper, we tend to create a different monster—disks full of data, fragments, useless files, and backups we will never need.

Yet, you need a certain amount of protection for these files as well, special "vault" duplicate backup disks that contain copies of your daily updates, archives, and other materials that can get your business back up and running even if a fire guts your office.

WHY ARCHIVE DUPLICATES?

In the good old days of doing everything on a typewriter and an adding machine, we would never have dreamed of keeping running duplicates of all the paperwork in a vault. It was too costly, too time-consuming, and too many other things that just made it less than feasible.

Then came microfilm—which lends itself admirably to keeping track of a ton of old documents, but lacks the timeliness of archiving yesterday's outgoing contracts and business mail.

A computer disk is a quick and easy way to keep archives (see Fig. 14-1). Where you keep such duplicates is up to you. A safety deposit box may be convenient, but hardly necessary. Unless the information on the disk is extremely sensitive, you can keep such disks *any-where*—other than in your present office building. The idea is to protect them from disaster, most notably a fire. You can throw the

Fig. 14-1. The typed author's manuscript for this book and the handful of minifloppy disk-ettes that hold all of the chapters, duplicate backup files, illustration lists, captions, credits, etc. With even more careful file management, the number of disks used could have been even further reduced.

vault duplicates in your briefcase or purse and take them home with you, if they're your responsibility.

Preparing the archive duplicates is another matter. If you use certain kinds of codes in your filenames, making archive copies becomes an easy chore.

In earlier chapters, we recommended using a date code in the filename extension—FILENAME.603, for example, meaning June 3. Obviously, because of the three-digit limitation, when you get near the end of the year, you'll only be able to use the second digit of the month: 0 for October, 1 for November, and 2 for December.

Since this can get confusing with January and February following close behind (also 1 and 2), you can use a letter instead: N for November and D for December. Thus November 5 will be N05. This is up to you and your personal preference.

Using PIP to Make Archive Copies

The date codes are important, because by having them in place, you can instruct your computer to copy entire blocks of files with one simple command.

Using the PIP (Peripheral Interchange Program) command, copying a file like XYZLET02.603 from Disk A to Disk B, will ordinarily call for this command:

A⟩PIP B: = A:XYZLET02.603 **[Return]**

The file will be copied, and when it's done, A⟩ will appear on the screen again.

Note that you can only use PIP when you're in the Operating System (A⟩ or B⟩ on the screen). Also, the PIP.COM program file should be on the logged disk. If B⟩ is on the screen, PIP.COM should be on the B disk. If it isn't, but is on the A disk, you can relog to A by simply typing A: **[Return],** or you can call up the PIP command this way:

B⟩A:PIP B: = A:XYZLET02.603 **[Return]**

Ambiguous Characters

The manuals call the asterisk (*) and question mark (?) "ambiguous" characters. Don't let that word throw you. It just means that the symbols can be replaced by almost anything. Here's what those symbols can do.

When you use the *, CP/M interprets this to mean "all files." This can save a ton of typing instructions on the keyboard. However, each file name has two parts—the FILENAME and the EXTension. So a file name looks like this: FILENAME.EXT. It has a maximum of eight characters followed by a period, followed by a three-character (maximum) extension.

If you want to copy *all* files from Disk A to Disk B, you can type this:

A⟩PIP B: = A:*.* **[Return]**

If you want CP/M to verify the files—checking the copy against the original, type this instead:

A⟩PIP B: = A:*.*[V] **[Return]**

You *must* use the square brackets on this "verify" instruction [V].

Copying this way will take longer than copying without verification, so plan to go for a cup of coffee while the computer is busy copying and checking.

The computer will respond somewhat differently when you use the ambiguous "wild card" symbols. It will say:

COPYING-
XYZLET02.603

and so on, listing each file as it starts the copy and verification process (see Fig. 14–2). When the list is all done, you'll have a column of file names, and at the bottom will be good old A⟩ again.

Remember, that if you have an older file with the same file name as one that you PIP-copy, the new file will erase the old one, so be careful with that *.* command.

You don't have to use the *.* for copying all files. Suppose you just want to copy the files that were entered or updated on June 3. If you've been using the date-code extension that we've been urging here, then all you have to type is:

A⟩PIP B: = A:*.603 **[Return]**

```
A>PIP B:=A:*.*[V]

COPYING -
PIP.COM
STAT.COM
DDT.COM
SUBMIT.COM
XSUB.COM
SYSGEN.COM
ED.COM
LOAD.COM
ASM.COM
MOVCPM.COM
DUMP.COM
ASSIGN.COM
DISKUTIL.COM
DDISKUTL.COM
ICPM60.ASM
EBIOS.ASM
```

Fig. 14–2. Using the PIP command with ambiguous filematch symbols can result in a complex computer copying list like this one. It's a real time-saver.

This will copy *all* files with the "603" extension. Again, if you want verification checking, you can add the [V] to the file name before hitting the **[Return]** key.

Now let's look at that (?) "wild card." If you want to copy all files for the month of June, you could type this:

A⟩PIP B: = A:*.6?? **[Return]**

CP/M will plug in all files whose extensions begin with the numeral 6, and all will be dutifully copied.

Here's another variation on the (?) wild card. Suppose you want to copy *all* the files for the XYZ company. You could type this:

A⟩PIP B: = A:XYZ?????.* **[Return]**

This will copy files that begin with XYZ, and CP/M will substitute any letters and numbers that may exist for those question marks, including blank spaces. The * in the extension means that you'll get not only date codes, but the BAK files as well. If you don't want those BAK files, do this next:

A⟩ERA B:*.BAK **[Return]**

This will get rid of *all* the BAK files on Disk B. But you may want to keep all the BAK files *except* the ones for the XYZ company. So do this instead:

A⟩ERA B:XYZ?????.BAK **[Return]**

Again, the wild card key comes to the rescue and saves you a lot of work.

Once you have all the files neatly copied onto your archive disk, make a couple of printed copies of just what's on the disk. Turn your printer on with **[Ctl]** P and then type:

A⟩DIR B: **[Return]**

The printer will nicely print out a directory of the contents of Disk B (see Fig. 14-3). If you'd like to print out a more detailed listing

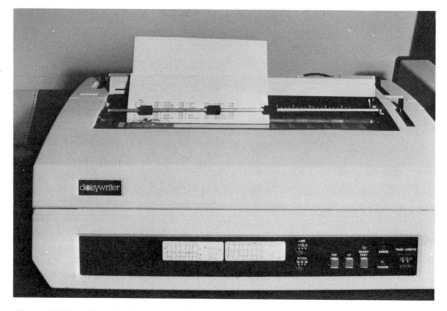

Fig. 14-3 (A). The disk directory (DIR) is handy on the screen. It's even handier if you print it out and store these printouts in a binder to make file finding faster and easier.

of the contents of the disk, and at the same time have a record of space used and space still available, with the printer turned on, type:

A〉STAT B:*.* **[Return]**

Keep a copy of this printout *in the jacket with the diskette* (see Fig. 14-4). If you like, you can use a three-hole punch and keep a copy of this printout in a binder with all your other pertinent disk

```
A〉DIR
A: PIP      COM : STAT      COM : DDT      COM : SUBMIT   COM
A: XSUB     COM : SYSGEN    COM : ED       COM : LOAD     COM
A: ASM      COM : MOVCPM    COM : DUMP     COM : ASSIGN   COM
A: DISKUTIL COM : DDISKUTL  COM : ICPM60   ASM : EBIOS    ASM
A:          PRN :           HEX :          COM : CRUN2    COM
A: CBAS2    COM : XREF      COM : WSU      COM : INSTALL  COM
A: EXAMPLE  TXT : WSMSGS    OVR : WSOVLY1  OVR : MPMPATCH COM
A: WS       COM
A〉
```

Fig. 14-3 (B). Printout of the disk directory using Control P in the Operating System, will look something like this.

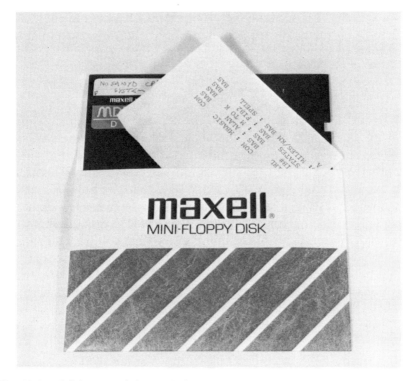

Fig. 14-4.   If disks get carried around a lot, keep a printout of the disk directory in the disk jacket. It'll save time and trouble.

information. Keeping such listings and directories is always a good idea, because this way you can find out what is where in an instant, instead of having to load and search disk directories one at a time.

UPDATING YOUR DISKS

As so often happens, you will find that you have more than one version of the same file. This can happen because of updates, revisions, and other changes that are a normal part of doing business.

Once a file has been used and has served its purpose, chances are you won't want to keep all the previous versions of it, but only the last, revised one. If you keep some kind of running record of these revisions in the filename or as a function of the date-code extension, you should be able to go through your disk directory and pick out the ones you no longer need. Erase them.

Use CP/M's ERA command, and get rid of these old files selectively or with the wild-card command keys. But do get rid of them. They take up valuable space that you can use for other files.

Conserving Disk Space

Bear in mind that in CP/M, even the shortest file occupies a minimum of 2K of disk space—whether it's one page or one sentence. Anything at all you can do in the interest of getting rid of "scrap" and practice files along with files of unneeded material will conserve disk space and make your own work flow that much easier.

But why conserve disk space? you may ask. If because you can buy quality diskettes for $3.00 each, you feel that disk conservation isn't needed, then bear this in mind: every time you have to change disks to get from one file to another, you waste *time*—time that you should be saving by using your computer effectively and efficiently.

You may also find that because of your open-handedness with the purchase of blank diskettes, you have related files spread all over the place. Files that may be used in conjunction with each other should be on the same disk, if at all possible. Very often you can't do this if you don't keep disks cleaned out and organized.

One common procedure is to use one disk as a "daily"—entering all new material for that day. At the end of the day, you transfer or copy files from your daily disk onto disks that contain complete files for a particular company or business. If you have correspondence for the XYZ Company and the JKL Company, for Acme Exterminators, Speedy Printers, and Bilt-Rite Locksmiths all on one disk, copy that XYZ file onto the XYZ Company disk. Sure, you may not have separate disks for the others, but keep as much material together as possible.

By the end of the week, if your daily disk is full of a lot of miscellaneous garbage that you want to keep for a while, print out a directory of the disk and put it aside as part of your in-house inactive disks. Whether or not you make an archive duplicate of this disk is up to you and how important you feel the material is.

BACKUP DISKS VS. BAK FILES

If you're confused by backup disks, backup files, and CP/M-generated backups, here's the story.

The CP/M Operating System will automatically create a separate backup file every time you save a file. It takes the regular filename and adds its own "BAK" extension to it. Thus, the file XYZLET02.603 gets a backup file name XYZLET02.BAK. Because of this, you can easily confuse both the computer and the CP/M system if you create two different files *with the same filename and different extensions.*

Thus, it would be bad business to create two different files named XYZLET01.603 and XYZLET01.604. When CP/M goes to make a backup file, which of these two files does it copy? Answer, whichever one is saved most recently, and the old BAK file will be erased, *even though it's for a different file.*

The solution to the dilemma: name the second file XYZLET02. 604. You still have the current date code intact in the file extension, and CP/M's backup file system won't be disrupted. If you want to get rid of the BAK files *after you've finished with a disk,* you can erase all the BAKs on Disk B with this command:

A)ERA B:*.BAK **[Return]**

Why does CP/M create BAK files? For your protection, in case something happens to your current, regular files, you always have the BAK of the most recent saved version. Since CP/M won't let you edit or print out BAK files, you can then make a copy of the BAK with some other extension. You can also read a BAK file into a WordStar file with the **[Ctl]** KR command. The BAK file system is there to help you, but these files can take an awful lot of disk space.

CARRYING DISKETTES

We suggested earlier that you put archive diskettes into your brief-case or purse for safekeeping. But there's a big danger in doing this—diskettes can easily get bent or creased in what can best be described as a hostile environment.

Invest a little money in heavy cardboard or reinforced plastic disk-ette mailers and use these for holding the floppies when you're car-rying them. A typical mailer can cost as little as 50 cents (see Fig. 14-5), and at prices like that, you can afford to be a big spender and go for the deluxe model for $2.00 or so.

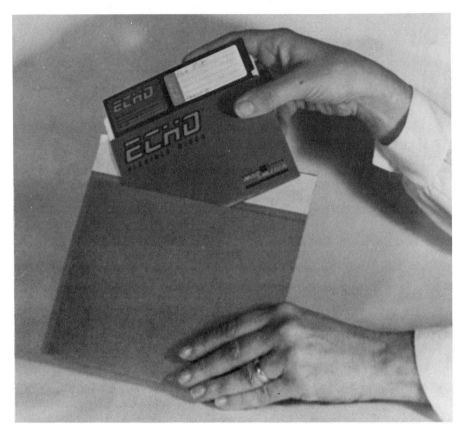

Fig. 14–5. If you're going to mail, send, or carry around floppy diskettes, invest in a few of these 50-cent protective mailers. They'll protect these delicate disks from the dangers of commuting, careless messengers, and sadistic postmen.

Also be careful of carrying diskettes through X-ray security machines in airports. If you're carrying diskettes, take them out of your bag and hand them to the security guard. You'll be a lot safer and a lot less sorry if you do. The X-rays won't hurt the disks, but X-ray machines generate lots of magnetism, and that's poison! But it's a small inconvenience to be sure that your records and files are kept intact. They'll do you no good if you get to your destination with damaged data.

15
Expanding Your Horizons

Once you get into the computer and its software, you'll begin to realize that there is other software out there—much of which can be a big help to you and to your business. After all, the computer represents a capital investment, and it doesn't pay for it to sit there doing nothing for a good part of the day.

If your management planners can use the computer to run out projections of figures and tables, it's helping to earn its keep. This is even more true if your bookkeeper can do billing, posting, receivables, payables, payroll, and all the other neat things that come out of that tight-money corner of the office.

What about adding to and expanding your word processing with spelling checkers? And why not add to your data base with more sophisticated and more dedicated programs for keeping records?

WORD PROCESSORS AND ENHANCEMENTS

Since you've read this far, you're probably well aware of word processing programs and what they can do. WordStar is probably one of the most versatile and well planned of this genre, and you're to be congratulated that you (1) have not only acquired WordStar for your computer, but (2) are also trying to learn how to use it. It's not as easy word processor to learn, but once you begin to feel even the slightest bit comfortable with it, you'll wonder how you ever got along without it. This entire book was written on a microcomputer using WordStar, and the author didn't consider for one moment using any other way of writing it.

An important enhancement for WordStar, already covered in previous chapters, is MailMerge. If you don't have this for your WordStar, get it immediately. It's dirt cheap (about $150), and relieves you and your secretaries of a ton of work and drudgery.

MailMerge works as an integral part of WordStar and is added to your master system disk in the form of *overlays*. Overlays are special files that can be addressed (called up) by the main WordStar program any time your commands call for it.

Another co-program for WordStar is SpellStar and a number of other spelling checkers—such as The Word, Spellguard, Random House Proofreader, Series 9 Spelling, and others of this type. Most CP/M spelling checkers will work in conjunction with WordStar, although if you use anything other than MicroPro's SpellStar, you can't activate them from the Main Menu with the ''S'' command. Instead, some other kind of command structure is used—usually outside the file after it has been saved and you have exited to the CP/M Operating System.

Some of these spelling checkers work very quickly and automatically, while others work methodically, checking each and every word in a file against a master ''dictionary.'' While the computer does this checking very quickly, it has to look up *each* word, and this can take an appreciable length of time—even for a relatively short file. This is the ideal time to go find that cup of coffee or do something else around the office.

Spread Sheets

They pose under a lot of different names, such as VisiCalc, SuperCalc, CalcStar, UltraCalc, PerfectCalc—*et al.*—but they're all called *Spread Sheets* and their existence is an absolutely wonderful reason for owning a computer.

A Spread Sheet can be regarded as a super bookkeeping ledger page—one with a couple of hundred lines and perhaps 75 or more columns (see Fig. 15-1). These are the outside or maximum dimensions; rarely do people really use all those columns and lines.

The wonderful thing about a Spread Sheet is that it allows you to enter interrelated data, and perform complex operations with the numbers—all automatically. If a new number entered in column F, line 27 will affect 20 other entries, the Spread Sheet program will

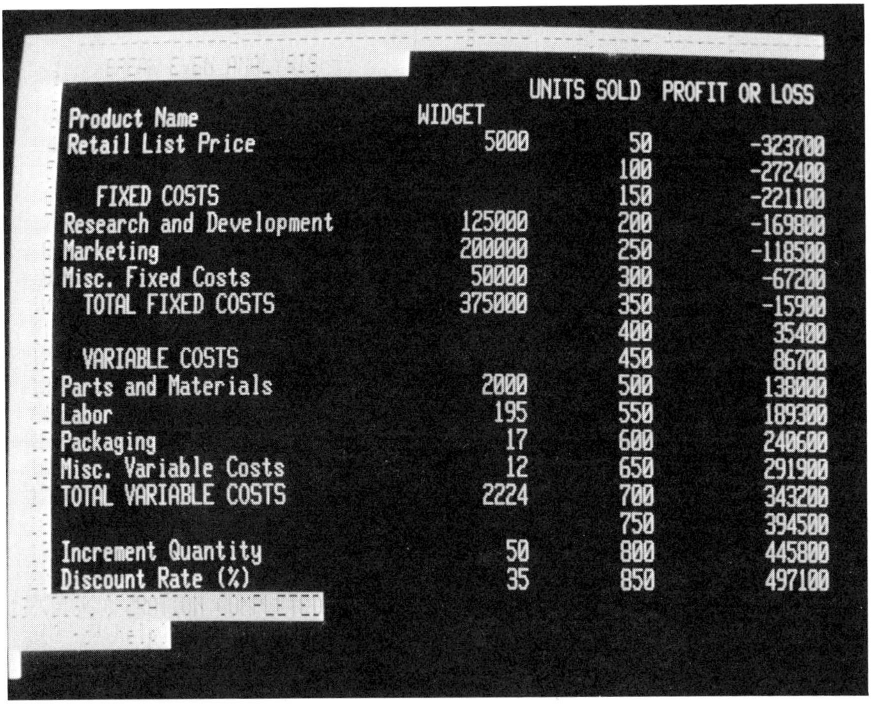

Fig. 15-1. A typical spread sheet (Ultracalc by Lattice, Inc. is shown here) is the second most useful applications program for your microcomputer. The screen display here is just a tiny piece of one corner of a "ledger sheet" that can extend to 64 columns of data and 255 rows of entries. Other spread sheets offer similarly large potential operating ranges.

make all the appropriate changes and adjustments in a wink. That in itself is a big time-saver.

Because of this feature, Spread Sheets are often called the "What If?" software. They let you try out different facts, figures, and parameters to see what would happen. As such, they become not only a powerful bookkeeping and financial record-keeping tool—they're also excellent for forecasting and making projections.

A typical Spread Sheet lets you save or print out either the entire sheet or any particular portion of it that you specify. You can print out just the information displayed on the computer screen, or you can print just one column or two, or any set of data you specify.

And they're easy to use, provided your software comes with a half-way decent tutorial. There are no quick-and-dirty ways to get on line with a Spread Sheet. Use the tutorial and work your way through the samples and examples they give you. You'll be an "expert" in an hour or two, and by then, you'll start to wonder how you ever got along without this wonderfully simple and detailed program. Try it; you'll *love* it!

Data Base Management

We've talked about data bases rather offhandedly in other parts of this book. It's not something designed to scare you off; in fact, you probably have dozens of data bases of your own already without realizing it. A data base is simply any collection of facts and figures about people or companies or other entities. In its simplest form, a data base is a Rolodex file or a desktop telephone directory of frequently called numbers.

With a computer and a data base management program, you can enter all these neat goodies into a disk file (or files) and do all kinds of wonderful things with them—such as printing out mailing labels, doing computerized individually typed form letters, updating cards for your Rolodex (if you wish), getting special phone list printouts for certain parts of the country when you're leaving on a business trip . . . the possibilities are almost endless.

A data base program can be something detailed like MicroPro's InfoStar—which is really a combination of DataStar and Report-Star. It can be created as part of Perfect Software's Perfect Filer; it can be something like Micro Lab's Data Factory or Mini Factory; or there are Ashton-Tate's dBaseII, dBaseIII, and Friday! programs—also excellent managerial-type data bases.

It's possible to create a data base without having a specific data base program for it, but it's just that much harder to do. When you use a prepared data base program, you can create prompt and question templates that ask you for specific information. The software never leaves blank fields unmarked; it can rearrange its components to suit whatever type of printout or screen display you need; and it will do sorting and selection for you without your having to go through a lot of keyboard gymnastics.

Graphics in the Office

Graphics require a very specific kind of software, and certain programs can take raw data from a Spread Sheet or other numerical input and create charts and graphs for you to use at your next sales meeting or presentation.

Some of the data base programs include a routine for creating graphs for you, while others may be tied to graphic generators. The vast majority of these are created for use with monochrome monitors and conventional dot-matrix-type printers.

But some graphics programs include color capability, and these can be real eye-zappers when you have a color monitor. The results can be converted to hard copy with the use of a special printout device called a *printer/plotter*. This machine uses special ball-point or ink-flow pens to draw continuous lines and shapes on a blank sheet of paper.

Many of these are equipped with pens of four or more colors, and your software can specify different colors for various parts of the chart or drawing. The drawing arm moves to the side of the printer/plotter and automatically changes pens when a different color is called for (see Fig. 15-2). Printer/plotters are fascinating to watch in operation; they're relatively inexpensive; and they're slow as the devil—usually tying up your computer for a half-hour at a time or more while a drawing is being plotted.

Some of them can, like printers, be used in conjunction with an external add-on buffer—a memory storage device that can take the entire file from the computer in one fast gulp, and drive the plotter or printer, while your computer is freed up to perform other tasks. If you need your computer on line and running all the time, then one of these external buffers (see Fig. 15-3) is really a must. And they're not all that expensive—typically retailing for about $175 to $400, depending on the memory size.

PROGRAMS FOR PROGRAMMING

Many computers come with some kind of programming language included on a disk. This is most often some form of BASIC, or more specifically, it's probably MicroSoft BASIC (MBASIC), which is the

Fig. 15-2. A printer/plotter uses special ball-point pens in any needed color to create computer-generated charts, graphs, and other graphics quickly and accurately. (*Photo courtesy Amdek Corp.*)

most popular form of this language for small business-type computers.

Don't be afraid to use MBASIC. It's a very powerful (although slow-moving) tool for creating and running programs of your own. But there are two different types of software related to programming languages. What you are likely to get with your computer is called an "Interpreter."

This type of program, when loaded, lets you type a list of programming instructions in the form of BASIC (for which it's designed). When you RUN the program, the interpreter reads each line and translates it into machine language—that strange binary language of ones and zeros that the computer needs in order to understand what you're talking about. Results are reinterpreted back into BASIC or into plain English so you know what the computer is talking about.

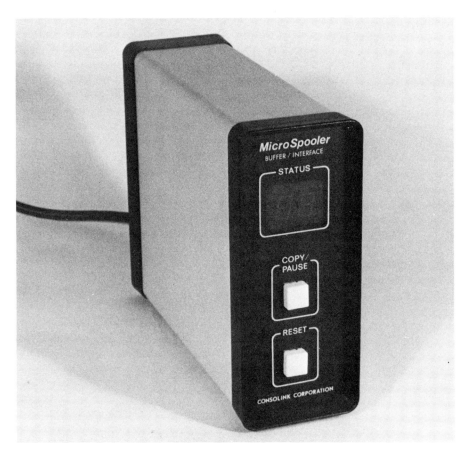

Fig. 15-3.   An external printer buffer like this MicroSpooler from Consolink Corp. can add huge amounts of memory to the printer, freeing up the computer to do other tasks while a print-out is in progress. This buffer is serial type, and adds 64K of memory to the printer—enough for two chapters of this book.

Obviously, the program would run much faster if it could be "crunched" into machine code and stored and used that way. That's where the *Compiler* comes in. This type of software is very expensive, and because of this, is rarely used by the casual programmer. The compiler takes each line of the BASIC program and makes a permanent translation of it in machine code in a separate file that you save and use.

Machine-code programs run at a fast and furious pace. Watching a compiler take your BASIC and work on it line by line is another experience that happens all too rarely. Just creating a successful program in BASIC and getting it "debugged" so it will run in the first place seems like a Herculean accomplishment. To see it get expertly crunched into machine code is just a little mind blowing. And some compilers let you watch them work—giving you machine language equivalents on the screen for each line before entering it into storage.

Appendix I
Do This First—Protect Your
Software with Backup Copies

The one thing you can damage in your computer is the information on the floppy disks. You have a set of software on "distribution" disks supplied by the manufacturer. There are at least two of these disks, possibly more.

- One of them contains CP/M and its utility programs.
- Another contains WordStar.
- Others may contain other software that you received with your computer.

THE FIRST THING YOU MUST DO is to make *backup* copies of those precious disks so they don't get damaged or destroyed. You are not violating any copyright laws, since the copies you make are for your own use and to protect your own property—the software that came with your computer.

Get a good supply of blank disks—at least two boxes (of 10 each). Buy a brand that you or your expert friends feel is reliable. We won't make any distinctions here, but good, reliable brands include: BASF, Dysan, Maxell, Radio Shack, TDK, 3M, and Verbatim. There are many others that we have not personally tested that are at least as good as these.

Also, some of the "better" brands, for some strange reason, don't match up too well with certain makes and models of computer. Yet they'll work just fine with other computer brands. There's no logical explanation for this; we just know it happens. So ask for some guid-

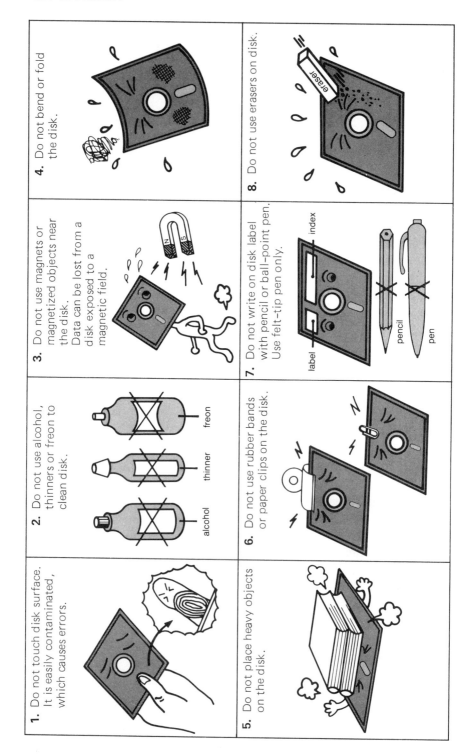

1. Do not touch disk surface. It is easily contaminated, which causes errors.

2. Do not use alcohol, thinners or freon to clean disk.

alcohol   thinner   freon

3. Do not use magnets or magnetized objects near the disk.
Data can be lost from a disk exposed to a magnetic field.

4. Do not bend or fold the disk.

5. Do not place heavy objects on the disk.

6. Do not use rubber bands or paper clips on the disk.

7. Do not write on disk label with pencil or ball-point pen. Use felt-tip pen only.

index   label   pencil   pen

8. Do not use erasers on disk.

eraser

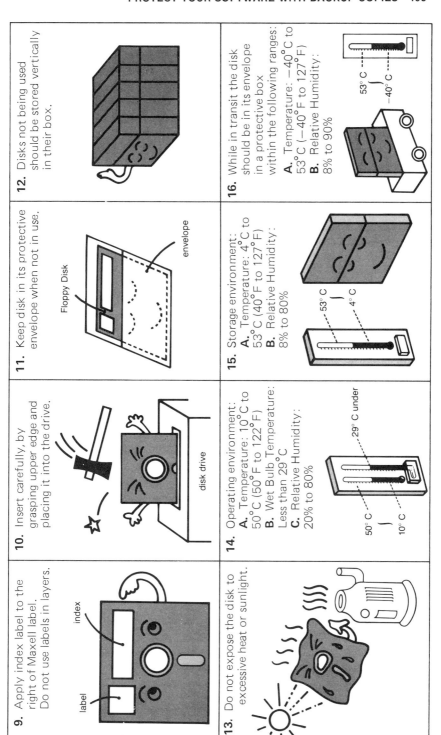

9. Apply index label to the right of Maxell label. Do not use labels in layers.

index
label

10. Insert carefully, by grasping upper edge and placing it into the drive.

disk drive

11. Keep disk in its protective envelope when not in use.

Floppy Disk
envelope

12. Disks not being used should be stored vertically in their box.

13. Do not expose the disk to excessive heat or sunlight.

14. Operating environment:
A. Temperature: 10°C to 50°C (50°F to 122°F)
B. Wet Bulb Temperature: Less than 29°C
C. Relative Humidity: 20% to 80%

29° C under
50° C
10° C

15. Storage environment:
A. Temperature: 4°C to 53°C (40°F to 127°F)
B. Relative Humidity: 8% to 80%

53° C
4° C

16. While in transit the disk should be in its envelope in a protective box within the following ranges:
A. Temperature: −40°C to 53°C (−40°F to 127°F)
B. Relative Humidity: 8% to 90%

53° C
−40° C

Fig. A–1.   Maxell floppy disk handling and storage precautions to protect against possible failure. (*Courtesy Maxell Corporation of America.*)

ance from your computer dealer in this area; and if you hear even one person bad-mouthing a particular disk brand, try to find out why. The dedicated computer user is often the most trustworthy source of information about product quality.

ONE STEP AT A TIME

There are three different operations involved in making a backup or copy diskette when you start with a blank or reusable disk:

- FORMATTING the blank disk, which creates pie-slice-shaped wedges called "sectors" that have magnetic markers for boundaries.
- COPYING the files from the master or "source" disk to the blank, formatted disk. Optional automatic verification (error checking) can be part of this operation.
- WRITING CP/M Operating System to the outer three tracks of the disk. These three tracks are always reserved for the Operating System.

A basic CP/M utility disk will contain three separate programs to perform these three functions:

Program Name	Function
FORMAT. COM	Formats the blank disk
PIP.COM	Copies files and verifies
SYSGEN.COM	Writes CP/M to System tracks

USING SPECIAL COPY PROGRAMS FOR MAKING BACKUP DISKS

Some CP/M utility disks may contain a special program that does all three duplicating operations with just one or two keystroke commands. The most common name for this program is COPY.COM or DISKUTIL.COM. Not all versions of these copy programs will perform all three of these operations. Some may perform just the formatting and the copying, and you still have to call up the SYSGEN program to write CP/M to the System tracks. Disks that contain such special programs may or may not also contain files named FORMAT.COM and SYSGEN.COM.

Okay, here goes. Follow these steps to make a safety set of backup disks before you do anything else.

1. Turn on the computer.
2. Find the disk that says "CP/M and Utilities" or "CP/M System Disk" or "CP/M Version 2.2" or something similar on its label.
3. Handle this disk and all disks carefully; do not touch any of those holes or openings, but handle only the black cardboard sleeve. Put the disk into the computer's "A" drive or "No. 1" drive. If the drive is horizontal, insert with the disk label facing up. If the drive is vertical, the label should face left. Insert the disk so the label goes in *last*.
4. The disk may or may not "click" into place; don't force it, just push enough so it goes all the way in.
5. Latch the door. Since there are at least four or five different kinds of disk drive door latches, we won't try to tell you how to do this. We have to assume that you saw some kind of demonstration at the store before you bought the computer.
6. *Boot* the system. All this may require is for you to push the "Reset" button; or, you may find that on your computer, you may have to press two or three particular keys on the keyboard at the same time. On some computers, merely inserting the disk in the drive and latching the door will do the trick. If the Reset button doesn't do it, check the manual or call your dealer and ask him about doing a "cold boot."
7. The disk drive will click and groan, and after a few seconds, the screen will announce:

KAYPRO II 64k CP/M vers 2.2

or something similar, depending on the computer and the version of CP/M you have.
8. Just below that, you'll see this:

A⟩[]

The [] is a blinking square or a blinking underscore line _. This is called the "cursor" and is your place marker. The cursor travels across the screen as you type.

The **A >** is called "A prompt" and it means the computer's CP/M is ready and waiting for you.
9. Now, before you do anything else, load a new blank diskette into the second disk drive—Drive B. Even though it's blank, it'll have a label on it so you can tell which end is up.

10. Type DIR and hit the **[Return]** or "Enter" key. "Return" means "enter" on a computer.
11. You'll now see a display of several columns of file names. These are the *utility* programs on the disk. See if there's one that says "COPY" or something like that. Many computer manufacturers have made your life easier by making up special copy programs that perform several complex CP/M operations for you—all with a single keystroke.

INSTRUCTION SET A
USING THE "COPY" UTILITY PROGRAM SUPPLIED WITH MANY COMPUTERS

IF THE COPY PROGRAM DOES EVERYTHING ELSE BUT WRITE CP/M TO THE DISK, THEN USE THE NEXT SET OF DIRECTIONS (INSTRUCTION SET B)

---

1. Invoke this program by typing COPY **[Return]** (or whatever name the computer manufacturer has given to his version of this program).

   The utility will come up on the screen with a menu of several choices and a number or letter for each one. Read the information displayed on the screen to see which you want. If there is an option that provides copying Disk A to Disk B with formatting, use that one. Press the letter you want—typically "C" for Copy.
2. If the program does NOT provide formatting with the copying, you must first format the blank disk in a separate operation. Don't worry about what formatting means for now. If there's no COPY program, or if it does not include formatting, skip the rest of this and go directly to INSTRUCTION SET C.

   The Copy program on your computer may also provide another feature: it will write the CP/M system to the blank disk after all the copying is finished. That's fine. Let it. It saves you work.
3. When all this is done, follow the directions that ask if you want to copy another diskette. Answer "Y" for Yes, or whatever else signifies yes.
4. Remove the no-longer-blank diskette, and USING A FELT-TIPPED MARKER ONLY, write "CP/M System Disk" on

the label. Put it in its jacket and put it aside for now. Also remove the master CP/M disk from Drive A and put it in its jacket. The copy program from this disk is still in the computer's memory and will be used to copy the other disks.

5. Put the WordStar master disk in Drive A and another blank disk in Drive B. DO NOT REBOOT THE COMPUTER. DO NOT PRESS THE RESET BUTTON.

6. Following the directions in the Copy program routine, copy the WordStar master disk. When finished, remove the new WordStar disk, and again, using a felt-tipped marker, write "WordStar System Disk" on the label. Put this and the master disks in their jackets and put them aside.

7. Repeat this operation for any other master software disks that came with the computer until you have a complete set of duplicates.

INSTRUCTION SET B
USING A "COPY" UTILITY PROGRAM VERSION SUPPLIED WITH MANY COMPUTERS THAT DOES EVERYTHING ELSE BUT DOES NOT WRITE CP/M TO THE DISK'S SYSTEM TRACKS

---

1. Invoke this program by typing COPY **[Return]** (or whatever name the computer manufacturer has given to his version of this program).

    The utility will come up on the screen with a menu of several choices and a number or letter for each one. Read the information displayed on the screen to see which you want. If there is an option that provides copying Disk A to Disk B with formatting, use that one. Press the letter you want—typically "C" for Copy.

2. If the program does NOT provide formatting with the copying, you must first format the blank disk in a separate operation. Don't worry about what formatting means for now. If there's no COPY program, or if it does not include formatting, skip the rest of this and go directly to INSTRUCTION SET C right now.

3. When all this is done, follow the directions that ask if you want to copy another diskette. Answer "Y" for Yes, or whatever else signifies yes.

4. Remove the no-longer-blank diskette, and USING A FELT-TIPPED MARKER ONLY, write "CP/M System Disk" on the label. Put it in its jacket and put it aside for now. Also remove the master CP/M disk from Drive A and put it in its jacket. The copy program from this disk is still in the computer's memory and will be used to copy the other disks.

5. Put the WordStar master disk in Drive A and another blank disk in Drive B. DO NOT REBOOT THE COMPUTER. DO NOT PRESS THE RESET BUTTON.

6. Following the directions in the Copy program routine, copy the WordStar master disk. When finished, remove the new WordStar disk, and again, using a felt-tipped marker, write "WordStar System Disk" on the label. Put this and the master disks in their jackets and put them aside.

7. Repeat this operation for any other master software disks that came with the computer until you have a complete set of duplicates.

8. Put the CP/M Master (original) System Disk back into Drive A and reboot the system—either with the Reset button or with a **[Ctl]** C.

9. Type SYSGEN **[Return]**

10. The computer will say something like this:

SYSGEN VERSION 2.2.B
SOURCE DRIVE NAME (OR RETURN TO SKIP)

11. Type the letter A

12. It will then say:

SOURCE ON A, THEN TYPE RETURN.

13. Hit the **[Return]** key.

14. The computer will then ask,

DESTINATION DRIVE NAME? (OR RETURN TO REBOOT)

15. Type the letter B

16. The computer will then say:

DESTINATION ON B, THEN TYPE RETURN.

17. Hit the **[Return]** key.

18. The computer will complete the operation in about three seconds and then the screen will say:

FUNCTION COMPLETE
DESTINATION DRIVE NAME (OR RETURN TO REBOOT)

19. Remove the formatted and sysgen-copied disk from Drive B, put in another formatted disk and go back to Step 15.
20. Repeat this operation until all of your formatted and copied backup disks have been through the SYSGEN process. This puts the CP/M Operating System on special outside-edge tracks that are reserved for this use.
21. When finished, remove each new disk, and USING A FELT-TIPPED MARKER ONLY, write "CP/M System Disk" on the label. Put this and the master disks in their jackets and put them aside.

INSTRUCTION SET C
THE FOLLOWING STEPS ARE ONLY FOR COMPUTERS THAT ARE NOT EQUIPPED WITH ANY KIND OF "COPY" UTILITY PROGRAM OTHER THAN FORMAT.COM, PIP.COM, AND SYSGEN.COM.

---

1. IF YOUR CP/M DISK DOES NOT HAVE A COPY PROGRAM ON IT, check the DIR listing to see if there are programs with these names: FORMAT.COM, PIP.COM, SYSGEN.COM. These three programs will do the same job as the COPY program, but it will take a little more work and they must each be run separately.
2. Put a blank disk in Drive B and type FORMAT **[Return]**
3. The screen will display several prompts, statements and questions about the Format procedure. It will warn you that formatting will erase anything now on the disk in Drive B. When you're ready, follow the directions, ending up with a **[Return]**. This will start the operation. Some computers just wink at you with the blinking cursor while the B Drive creaks and groans. Other computers may show you something is going on by flashing track numbers or letters, or asterisks across the screen—just something to keep your eyes occupied while the formatting is being done.
4. When it's finished, it will ask you if you want to repeat the operation for another disk. Remove the formatted blank disk

and replace it with another blank. You will repeat the process with this disk and with as many blanks as you need for your software masters. If you have four masters, format four blanks.

5. When all of your blanks have been formatted, leave the last one in the drive, and holding down the "CONTROL" (or "CTL") key, type the letter C. This will give you a "Warm Boot" and A⟩ will once again appear on your screen.

6. Type PIP **[Return]**

7. The PIP copying program will load and you'll see an asterisk prompt on the screen: * with the cursor flashing right next to it.

8. Type the following EXACTLY with just the right spaces and punctuation in the right places:

   B: = A:*.*[V] **[Return]**

9. The word, **COPYING-** will appear on the screen, and under that will appear the name of the first file it copies, then under that the second, and so on, until PIP copies every file from Disk A to Disk B. The [V] tells it to verify everything by checking the copied file against the original as it goes along.

10. When it's all done, another asterisk (*) will appear. Remove the disk from Drive B, label it "CP/M System Disk" with a FELT TIPPED MARKER and put it aside for the moment.

11. With the asterisk still on the screen, put another blank **FOR-MATTED** disk into Drive B and put the WordStar master disk into Drive A.

12. Repeat step 8 and the steps that follow. Do this for each master disk that came with the computer until you have a complete set.

AFTER YOU HAVE DONE THIS WITH EACH DISK, PUT THE CP/M SYSTEM MASTER DISK BACK IN DRIVE A, AND ONE OF YOUR NEWLY COPIED DISKS IN DRIVE B.

13. Type **[Ctl]** C, and when the A> appears, type SYSGEN **[Return]**

14. The computer will say something like this:

SYSGEN VERSION 2.2.B
SOURCE DRIVE NAME (OR RETURN TO SKIP)

15. Type the letter A
16. It will then say:

SOURCE ON A, THEN TYPE RETURN.

17. Hit the **[Return]** key.
18. The computer will then ask,

DESTINATION DRIVE NAME? (OR RETURN TO REBOOT)

19. Type the letter B
20. The computer will then say:

DESTINATION ON B, THEN TYPE RETURN.

21. Hit the **[Return]** key.
22. The computer will complete the operation in about three seconds and then the screen will say:

FUNCTION COMPLETE
DESTINATION DRIVE NAME (OR RETURN TO REBOOT)

23. Remove the formatted and sysgen-copied disk from Drive B, put in another formatted disk, and repeat from Step 19.
24. Repeat this operation until all of your formatted blank disks have been through the SYSGEN process. This puts the CP/M Operating System on special outside-edge tracks that are reserved for this use.
25. Leave the last disk in place and hit **[Return]** again. The system will reboot, and you'll see **A>** on the screen.

NOW PUT THOSE MASTER DISKS AWAY IN A SAFE PLACE AND FORGET THAT THEY'RE THERE. USING THE SAME PROCEDURES THAT YOU USED TO MAKE THESE BACK-UPS, MAKE NEW COPIES OF THE NEW BACKUP DISKS ONTO OTHER DISKS WHICH YOU WILL USE AS "WORKING DISKS." KEEP THE NEW BACKUP DISKS IN A SAFE PLACE IN THE OFFICE TO MAKE NEW WORKING DISKS WHEN-EVER THEY'RE NEEDED.

Appendix II
Single-Page Letter Format

Now here's the drill for setting up a single-spaced single-page letter with 12-pitch type (for 10-pitch, omit **[Ctl]** PA **[Return]**:
If you are in WordStar's "No-File" or "Main" Menu:

Type the letter "D".
Screen will ask: "NAME OF FILE TO EDIT"
Type *complete and correct* file name and **[Return]**.
WAIT
Type .OP **[Return]**
Type **[Ctl]** PA **[Return]**
Stroke **[Ctl]** OJ
Stroke **[Ctl]** OH
Stroke **[Ctl]** ON
Type A **[Return]**
Stroke **[Ctl]** OI
Type 6 **[Return]**
Stroke **[Ctl]** OI
Type 41 **[Return]**

Now you're ready to start typing.

Appendix III
Getting Into WordStar

Fire up your computer.

Put a WordStar/systems disk in Drive A.

Put a blank, formatted file disk in Drive B.

If your system is self-booting, A⟩ will appear on the screen.

If your system is not self-booting, press the RESET button.

A⟩ should appear.

Type WS **[Return]**.

The computer will click and groan, the screen will go blank for a few seconds, and then the first WordStar message will appear on the screen along with a lot of information about copyright.

WAIT.

After a few more seconds, the disk drives will click and groan again, and the WordStar protocol will come up on the screen, listing your computer or a lookalike, the printer or equivalent, and the type of communications protocol.

WAIT.

After a few seconds more, the WordStar No-File Menu will appear along with a directory of the files on that disk.
At this point, you are logged into Drive A—the system/programs disk.

You want to log into Drive B.

Hit "L"

A prompt will appear telling you to type the Drive letter and a colon.

Type: B: **[Return]** (that's a *colon,* not a semi-colon—use the SHIFT key)

A new directory will come up under the menu labeled Disk B. You're ready to create your first file.

Appendix IV
File Setup

To set the typing parameters you need, do the following:

[Ctl] OJ turns off right-margin justification to give you ragged right.

[Ctl] OH turns off hyphen-help for greater speed in reformatting.

[Ctl] OR lets you reset the right margin. You might want to leave it alone your first couple of times around.

[Ctl] OS lets you change from single-spacing to double-, triple- or whatever spacing you want up to nine spaces.

If you want to change TAB stops, which are set every five spaces on the ruler line at startup, first CLEAR the old TAB stops.

Hit **[Ctl]** ON

WordStar will ask you which stops to clear.

Type "A" **[Return]**

This will clear *all* TAB stops.

Now suppose you want to set TABS at columns 6 and 41—good for paragraph indents and for tabbing to type a date, letter close, etc.

Hit **[Ctl]** OI, then the number 6 **[Return]**

Hit **[Ctl]** OI again, then the number 41 **[Return]**

If you're setting up a table and want to set TAB stops at column headings, move the cursor to the first column heading, hit **[Ctl]** OI and then **[Escape]**. This will set the TAB at the cursor location.

Appendix V
File Operations

The K menu works with block operations. Here are the file commands:

[Ctl] KS—saves the file without exiting. After the save is completed, you can return to your original cursor location with **[Ctl]** QP.

[Ctl] KD—saves the file and exits to the No-File (Main) Menu.

[Ctl] KX—saves the file and exits from WordStar to the operating System, giving you the A⟩ or B⟩.

[Ctl] KQ—abandons the file and doesn't save any changes.

[Ctl] KJ—deletes a file other than the one you're working on.

[Ctl] KO—lets you copy a file external to the one you're working on.

[Ctl] KR—lets you read another file into the file you have open.

[Ctl] KW—lets you copy a marked block to another, external file.

[Ctl] KP—lets you print any file without exiting from the file you're working on. You may also print the file you're working on in its last saved version.

[Ctl] KE—lets you rename another file.

Appendix VI
Quick-Key Operations

The Q or "Quick" menu lets you do a number of special operations. The **[Ctl]** Q keys *always* work in combination with some other key, so we'll be showing double letters here.

[Ctl] QS—moves cursor to far left end of line.

[Ctl] QD—moves cursor to far right end of line.

[Ctl] QR—moves cursor to beginning of the file.

[Ctl] QC—moves cursor to end of the file.

[Ctl] QY—deletes entire line to the right of the cursor.

[Ctl] Q-DEL—deletes entire line to the left of the cursor.

[Ctl] QF—find.

[Ctl] QA—find and replace.

[Ctl] QE—moves cursor to top of screen.

[Ctl] QX—moves cursor to bottom of screen.

[Ctl] QQ—repeats command; speed can be varied by tapping numeral.

[Ctl] QL—find misspelled word (only if you have SpellStar program).

[Ctl] Q1—find place marker ⟨1⟩

Appendix VII
Print Commands

The "P" or Print menu has many two-key controls that appear on the screen as a control caret and just one letter: ^S, ^B, etc. Many of these are useful during actual writing. With some of them, you have to turn the function on and off—such as ^S (underscore) and ^B (boldface). Here's a summary:

[Ctl] PS—(on/off) underscores all *typed* material, but not spaces.

[Ctl] PB—(on/off) boldfaces.

[Ctl] PD—(on/off) doublestrikes characters.

[Ctl] PV—(on/off) subscript characters.

[Ctl] PT—(on/off) superscript characters.

[Ctl] PX—(on/off) strikeout characters (with slashes).

[Ctl] PH—overprints single character (useful for foreign accents).

[Ctl] PM—overprints entire line (useful for underscoring).

[Ctl] PC—makes printer pause and wait for resume command (useful for changing typewheels).

Appendix VIII
Vendors Mentioned in this Book

When you're just beginning, it's sometimes hard to put names together with companies. If you have read about a particular product in this book that interests you, and your local computer store has no information, feel free to write or call the vendor (manufacturer) directly. They'll usually be only too happy to send you literature and direct you to a retail store near you that handles their products.

For your convenience, here's a list of sources. It's really only a starter set. There are thousands of manufacturers of computers, software, and supplies in the United States.

VENDOR LIST

Amdek Corp.
2201 Lively Blvd.
Elk Grove, IL. 60007
(312)364-1180
Products: Monitors, Printers, Disk Drives

Apple Computer
20525 Mariani Avenue
Cupertino, CA. 95014
(408)996-1010
Products: Computer Systems

Brother International
8 Corporate Place
Piscataway, NJ. 08854
(201)981-0300
Products: Printers

Bush Industries Inc.
312 Fair Oak Street
Little Valley, NY. 14755
(716)938-9101
Products: Furniture

Computers International
3540 Wilshire Blvd.
Los Angeles, CA. 90010
(213)386-3111
Products: Printers

Comrex International Inc.
3701 Skypark Drive
Torrance, CA. 90505
(213)373-0280
Products: Monitors, Printers, Disk Drives

Consolink Corp.
1840 Industrial Circle
Longmont, CO. 80501
(303)651-2014
Trademark: "MICROSPOOLER"
Products: External Buffers

Continental Software Co.
11223 South Hindry Avenue
Los Angeles, CA. 90045
(213)410-3977
Products: Software

Diablo Systems, Inc.
P.O. Box 5030
Fremont, CA. 94537
(415)498-7000
Products: Printers

Digital Research
P.O. Box 579
Pacific Grove, CA. 93950
(408)649-3896
Trademark: "CP/M"
Products: Software

Discwasher
P.O. Box 6021
Columbia, MO. 65205
(314)499-0941
Products: Accessories

Dymarc Industries
21 Governor's Ct.
Baltimore, MD. 21207
(301)298-9626/(800)638-9098
Trademark: "CLIPSTRIP"
Products: Voltage Protectors

Dynax Inc.
5698 Bandini Blvd.
Bell, CA 90201
(213)260-7121
Products: Monitors, Printers

Eagle Computer
983 University Avenue
Los Gatos, CA. 95030
(408)395-5005
Products: Computer Systems

Epson America Inc.
3415 Kashiwa Street
Torrance, CA. 90505
(213)539-9140
Products: Computer Systems, Printers

Gusdorf Corp.
6900 Manchester Avenue
St. Louis, MO. 63143
(800)325-3622
Products: Furniture

IBM Dept. 8m3
P.O. Box 1328
Boca Raton, FL. 33432
(305)998-2000
Products: Computer Systems, Monitors,
Printers

Kaypro Corp.
533 Stevens Avenue
Solana Beach, CA. 92075
(714)755-1134
Products: Computer Systems, Printers

Leading Edge Products Inc.
225 Turnpike Street
Canton, MA. 02021
(617)828-8150
Products: Computer Systems, Monitors,
Printers, Blank Disks

Mag-Media Inc.
405 West College Avenue
Santa Rosa, CA. 95401
(707)578-3200/(800)858-8600
Trademark: "ECHO"
Products: Blank Disks

Maine Manufacturing Co.
P.O. Box 408
Nashua, NH 03061
(603)882-5142
Trademark: "DATA-MATE"
Products: Furniture

Maxell Corporation of America
60 Oxford Drive
Moonachie, NJ. 07074
(201)440-8020
Products: Blank Disks

MicroPro International Corp.
33 San Pablo Avenue
San Rafael, CA. 94903
(415)499-1200
Trademark: "WORDSTAR"
Products: Software

Microsoft Consumer Products
10700 Northrup Way
Bellevue, WA. 98004
(206)828-8080
Products: Software

Okidata
111 Gaither Drive
Mount Laurel, NJ. 08054
(609)235-2600
Products: Printers

O'Sullivan Industries Inc.
19th and Gulf Streets
Lamar, MO. 64759
(417)682-3322
Products: Furniture

Otrona Corp.
4755 Walnut Street
Boulder, CO. 80301
(303)444-8100
Products: Computer Systems

Radio Shack
1800 One Tandy Center
Fort Worth, TX. 76102
(817)390-3300
Products: Computer Systems, Monitors,
Printers, Software, Blank Disks, Supplies

Shugart Associates
475 Oakmead Parkway
Sunnyvale, CA. 94086
(408)733-0100
Products: Disk Drives

Software Publishing Corp.
1901 Landings Drive
Mountain View, CA. 94043
(415)962-8910
Trademark: "PFS"
Products: Software

Sola Electric/General Signal
1717 Busse Road
Elk Grove Village, IL. 60007
(312)439-2800
Products: Voltage Protectors

Star Micronics Inc.
P.O. Box 1630
El Toro, CA. 92630
(800)621-0212
Products: Printers

The 3M Company
3M Center
Saint Paul, MN. 55144
(612)733-1387/(800)328-9438
Products: Blank Disks, Anti-Static Mats

The Texwipe Co.
P.O. Box 308
Upper Saddle River, NJ 07458
(201)327-9100
Products: Cleaning Accessories

Appendix IX
Good Reading for the Beginning
Business Computer User

CP/M Primer by Stephen M. Murtha and
  Mitchell Waite
$14.95
Howard W. Sams & Co., Inc.
4300 W. 62nd Street
Indianapolis, IN 46268

The CP/M Handbook With MP/M by Rodney Zaks
$14.95
Sybex, Inc.
2344 Sixth Street
Berkeley, CA 94710

Doing Business with SuperCalc by Stanley R.
  Trost
$12.95
Sybex, Inc.
2344 Sixth Street
Berkeley, CA 94710

*DON'T! (Or How to Care For Your Com-
  puter)* by Rodney Zaks
$11.95
Sybex, Inc.
2344 Sixth Street
Berkeley, CA 94710

International Microcomputer Dictionary
$3.95

Sybex, Inc.
2344 Sixth Street
Berkeley, CA 94710

Introduction to WordStar by Arthur Naiman
$11.95
Sybex, Inc.
2344 Sixth Street
Berkeley, CA 94710

Mastering VisiCalc by Douglas Hergert
$11.95
Sybex, Inc.
2344 Sixth Street
Berkeley, CA 94710

Practical WordStar Uses by Julie Anne Arca
$13.95
Sybex, Inc.
2344 Sixth Street
Berkeley, CA 94710

The New American Computer Dictionary by
  Kent Porter
$3.50
The New American Library, Inc.
1633 Broadway
New York, NY 10019

Appendix X
Where To Buy Supplies

It's not always a simple matter to walk into your local computer store and walk out with just the right daisy wheel or ribbon or box of diskettes for your computer. Besides, they'll often charge you an arm and a leg.

Some catalog supply houses specialize in computer supplies by mail order—and some will take phone orders and charge it to your major credit card. Also, some of these suppliers offer considerable savings for quantity purchases. If you expect to use a lot of diskettes, for example, buy a case of 100 and get really good cost savings.

Here are just a few of these specialty catalog houses. You can call and write for their catalogs and can even place an order without having the catalog in front of you. Don't be bashful; you're a *customer*.

MAIL ORDER LISTINGS

DEVOKE DATA PRODUCTS
1500 Martin Avenue
Santa Clara, CA 95050
(408)980-1360

INMAC (Corporate Hdqtrs.)
2465 Augustine Drive
Santa Clara, CA 95051
(Orders taken at 14 regional offices; use phone number nearest to you.)
Sunnyvale, CA (408)737-7777
Irvine, CA (714)641-3100
Los Angeles, CA (213)852-0973
Dallas, TX (214)641-0024

Denver, CO (303)825-6568
Chicago, IL (312)885-8383
Detroit, MI (313)961-6865
Atlanta, GA (404)441-3041
Washington, D.C. (301)731-5980
Closter, NJ (201)767-3601
New York, NY (212)517-8715
Philadelphia, PA (215)567-4066
Hudson, NH (603)889-4900
Boston, MA (617)536-9141
US Territories (Order from nearest US branch)
Canada and Mexico (Call nearest US branch for details)

213

Germany and Continental Europe
  Inmac GmbH
  Frankfurter Strasse 103
  D-6096 Raunheim
  Federal Republic of Western Germany
  (FGR)06142-43003
United Kingdom and Middle East
  Inmac-UK, Ltd.
  18 Goddard Road
  Astmoor Industrial Estate
  Runcorn, Cheshire WA71QF,U.K.
  (United Kingdom) 09285 67551

Global Computer Supplies
9133 Hemlock Drive

Hempstead, NY 11550
(516)292-340/(800)645-6393

Misco
P.O. Box 399
Holmdel, NJ 07733
(201)946-3500/(800)631-2227

Computer Mail Order East
477 East Third Street
Williamsport, PA 17701
(717)327-9575/(800)233-8950

Index